Edizioni R.E.I. France

Mantelli - Brown - Kittel - Graf

Macchi M.C. 200
Macchi M.C. 202
Macchi M.C. 205

ISBN 978-2-37297-3649

Edizioni R.E.I. France
www.edizionirei.webnode.com
edizionireifrance@outlook.com

Mantelli - Brown - Kittel - Graf

Macchi M.C. 200
Macchi M.C. 202
Macchi M.C. 205

Edizioni R.E.I. France

Index

Macchi M.C. 200

The Macchi M.C.200 "Saetta" was a single-engine low-wing fighter aircraft developed by the Italian aeronautical company Aeronautica Macchi in the 1930s. He made his first flight on December 24, 1937 and entered online in 1939. Although equipped with a low-powered engine and armed with only a pair of 12.7 mm caliber machine guns, the design of the "Saetta" was very valid. The Macchi M.C.200 had no particular defects and was equipped with excellent skills for close combat.

In fact, its maneuverability was excellent and the stability in the high-speed beaten, exceptional. He could thus duel with the best allied fighters and get out of them unbeaten. Only the Supermarine Spitfire could overcome it, in cabrata. From the entry into the war of Italy, on 10 June 1940, at the armistice of 1943, the Saetta carried out more operational missions than any other Italian aircraft. With the insignia of the Regia Aeronautica, he worked on almost all the fronts of the Second World War, from the Mediterranean Sea, to Africa, to the Balkans. An Autonomous Group operated in Russia where it obtained an excellent knockdown/loss ratio of 88 to 15.

The C. 200 were built, as well as by the parent company Aer.Macchi (395 units), also by Breda, who actually built the greater number (556), and by the SAI Ambrosini (223), in different production lots; this determined small differences in the painting of aircraft, both from firm to company, and from different production series.

At a first, immediate examination, it is still possible to distinguish the aircraft manufacturer by examining the cross of Savoy at the tail, since each company adopted a different style for this sign:

- Breda aircraft were characterized by a cross with equal arms.
- Those of Macchi production had the vertical arm longer than the horizontal one.
- The planes that came out of the factories of SAI Ambrosini carried a cross similar to that Macchi, whose arms however extended upwards, downwards and backwards, up to the edge of the rudder (in Macchi aircraft, however, they were truncated).

History

After the experience in Spain with the Fiat C.R.32, during the Spanish civil war, the request of the pilots of faster and more modern means is soon received by the top of the Royal Air Force. For this purpose, on February 10, 1936, a specification was issued for the provision of a Terrestrial Interceptor Hatch that was to correspond to the following services and equipment:

- maximum speed of 500 km / h
- climb to 6,000 meters in 5 minutes
- two-hour autonomy
- armed with one or two 12.7 mm caliber machine guns
- low-wing monoplane wing configuration
- adoption of a retractable landing gear
- use for the Fiat A.74 radial engine propulsion.

The aircrafts presented are three: Macchi C.200, Fiat G.50, IMAM RO 51. The C.200 stravince, resulting by far the best and reporting a total score of "30", against "25" of the Fiat fighter and "16" of the RO 51. In the following years, other fighters will be examined by the Regia Aeronautica: RE 2000, F5, CR42. Despite this additional competition, the C.200 will constitute, until the entry into service of the Macchi C.202, in autumn 1941, the spearhead of the specialty, the only interceptor capable of confronting, on Malta and in the northern theater African, with British appliances. Macchi entrusts the project to the engineer Mario Castoldi; the C.200, sometimes named "Macchi-Castoldi", from which the acronym M.C., is a low-wing monoplane, a type of aircraft of which Ing. Castoldi already has a ten-year experience with his remarkable runs, such as the Macchi M.39, winner in the prestigious Schneider Cup of 1926 and, in 1931, with the very fast M.C.72, the first to officially carry the M.C.

Castoldi would have preferred to entrust the propulsion to an in-line engine, but the national motorsport production was now almost exclusively directed towards radials, which were also produced under license. In a short time he manages to make the first prototype, military brands MM.336, which will be taken to the air for the first time, from the Promed Field of Lonate Pozzolo, December 24, 1937, piloted by test pilot Giuseppe Burei. The luminaire is beautiful, with graceful lines, with an extremely curved engine cowling under the aerodynamic profile, characterized by the "bosses", or those typical undulations, observable at first sight, that enclose the cylinder heads. The cockpit is closed, in the aircraft of the first production series, by means of a sliding panel backwards. Subsequently, in most of the models produced, the passenger compartment will be of the semi-open type, equipped with side slits that can be pulled down on the sides of the fuselage.

First impressions are considered positive but, as far as it is successful, it is born with a defect of auto rotation. Already from the tests carried out on 11 June 1938 in Guidonia, by Major Ugo Borgogno, it was clear that the turn at 90 ° could not be much tightened because the apparatus tended to overturn on the opposite side, particularly on the right.

If the turn was too close, the Macchi entered a dangerous car rotation (high-speed stall, due to the detachment of the fluid vein from the wing with a constant profile). It was the same defect that also characterized the contemporaries Fiat G.50, IMAM Ro.51, in 1937, and the AUSA AUT 18 and Reggiane Re.2000, in 1939. At the beginning of 1940 two pilots were killed precisely because of this defect. Deliveries and flights were suspended. The plane is considered, by the average of the pilots, "not pilotable", just as an order of 12 airplanes for Denmark goes up in smoke, due to the German invasion.

The self-rotation of an aircraft consists in the phenomenon of detachment of the fluid vein near the ends of the wings. This generates a rotation of the aircraft itself around the roll axis, which, depending on the characteristics of the aircraft involved, can self-extinguish or be galvanized.

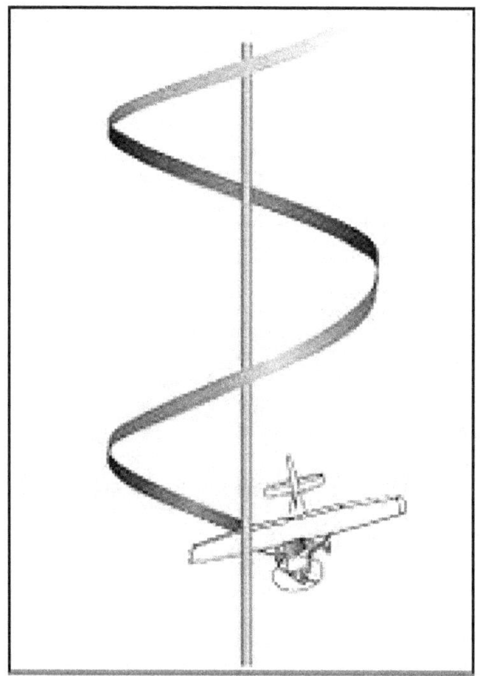

Grapevine - aggravated stall and self-rotation

This second event can lead to the ungovernability of the aircraft, since any attempt to correct the motion of self-rotation by means of the ailerons has the opposite effect of increasing the rotation speed of the airplane. When the wing is stalled and the angle of attack is greater than the stall angle, each increase in the angle of attack causes a descent of the climb coefficient with consequent descent of the aircraft. As the wing descends, the angle of attack increases, causing the rise coefficient to decrease and the angle of attack to increase. Thus reversing the terms.

For this reason the angle of attack is unstable when it is greater than the stall angle. Any variation of the angle of attack on a wing will cause the entire wing to rotate spontaneously and continuously. When the angle of attack of an aircraft wing reaches the stall angle, the aircraft is at risk of self rotation; it can degenerate into a rotation if the pilot does not implement corrective measures.

Another drawback is the poor rear visibility through the plexiglas of the canopy, due to the quality of the plastic laminate and to particular polarization phenomena of light on its surface. Similarly to what reported for the G. 50, the opening of the hood, beyond a certain speed, becomes impossible due to the aerodynamic depression. The solution of the open passenger compartment is therefore proposed again. But this happens on a date after December 1940, or after the first 240 units.

The first series of 99 aircraft (MM 4495-4593), has, in fact, left the company, starting from the summer of 1939. On November 10th 29 have already been delivered. Initially they flow to the 10th group of the 4th flock , but the aircraft, not well accepted by the pilots of this department already in the transition phase on the CR. 42, is transferred to the 6th group of the 1st flock hunt. In June 1940, the C. 200 are with the 6th group (Catania), with the 152nd (Airasca) and with the 153th group (Vergiate) of the 54th flock: a total of 144 aircraft. Shortly after the start of hostilities two fatal accidents occurred at the 1st flock, lead to the suspension of flights with this device. The subsequent investigation makes it possible to ascertain that it was the usual, notorious phenomena of self-rotation and in September the aircraft is operational again, in the sky of Malta: stocks to the MS. 79 and interception missions. The cause of the trouble of the M.C.200 was in the new wing profile. Castoldi immediately began experimenting with a new type of wing, but it was the engineer Sergio Stefanutti who found the solution simply by gluing layers of balsa plywood in the middle and at the ends.

Castoldi renounces the new wing, which will be reserved for Macchi MC. 202. Now the device inspires confidence to pilots, has a good general behavior in flight quality and acrobatics, even if in very tight turns to the right still tends to overturn, and is virtually free of vibration.

In this way the Macchi 200 was soon revealed as our best hunt of the time: its entry on the Greek-Albanian front confirmed it with numerous successes on the Hurricane, but, to save weight, the Macchi of the initial production had no armor for protect the pilot. Armorings often arrived at war, sometimes when the units were about to replace the "Saette" with the new Macchi M.C.202, and in any case in limited numbers. And after the armor had been mounted, centering the plane could be rather laborious and even dangerous. During acrobatic maneuvers, he could enter a flat vine from which the only way out was to launch himself with the parachute, as happened to Leonardo Ferrulli, on July 22nd, 1941, in Sicily.

The C.200, was in itself an excellent device, being however to serve a deficit of about 200 hp of power against the British fighters of the period, as well as being armed with only two 12.7 mm machine guns, while its counterparts foreigners are equipped with 8 wing guns or a mixed weaponry of 20 mm guns and cannons.

During the entire production period, 1.153 copies will be built, including the two prototypes MM.336 and MM.337, of M.C.200, realized in 24 different non-homogeneous lots from:

- Macchi - 395 plus prototypes
- Breda - 556
- Italian Aeronautica Ambrosini Company - 200.

Technique

The Macchi MC200 presented, like its counterpart Fiat G.50, a breakthrough in the Italian aeronautical production of the time, already undertaken unsuccessfully by Breda Ba.27, that of the adoption of a monoplane wing configuration and an entirely metallic structure . The fuselage was set on a shell structure with four duralumin side members assembled from trims in molded duraluminium segments.

The coating was in 'superavional' printed, riveted to the structure with riveting totally embedded, so as to constitute a surface with the least aerodynamic resistance. Between the two side members of the central part was placed in the lower area the main fuel tank (capacity 238 liters), while at the top were collected weapons, ammunition boxes and boxes collect shells. This was a characteristic of Italian fighters of the time: they did not want to disperse the precious metal material after the firing of weapons, accepting the penalization of unnecessary weight after the fight. Two opening doors at the top of the fuselage allowed the maintenance of the weapons.

Already in the first versions with a closed cockpit closed roof and in the following with the cockpit open, a special anti-scuffed resistant structure was built in the rear fairing of the passenger compartment. The front and back of the windshield was fixed, while the central one was mobile and allowed, in case of need, the launch with the parachute.

The bottles for the fire extinguisher, for the oxygen system and for start-up were placed just behind the cockpit, while a second fuel tank (capacity 75 liters) was located under the floor of the passenger compartment and was connected to the main with a flexible tube. Under the fuselage there were the connections for an additional external tank (capacity 150 liters) quickly removable; the position of the pilot was somewhat elevated and allowed him an excellent visibility. In the first series a reclosable canopy had been adopted but it was found to present the problem of the impossibility of opening beyond a certain speed due to pressurization; moreover there were less problems for the opacification of the transparent material of the rear part, so in the following series the half-open version was opted for. Posteriormente ended in a classic single-tailed fletching with horizontal cantilevered planes.

The empennages consisted of a fixed horizontal plane and a fixed vertical plane to which the rudders of depth and direction respectively followed. The side plates of the fixed and drift plan were of high strength steel tube, the ribs and the cover were in duralumin. The axle tube of the rudders of depth and direction was in steel, the ribs and the edges were in duralumin, the cover in canvas. The fixed plane was adjustable in flight, the rear side member was fixed with supports to the fuselage and these supports allowed the rotation of some degrees of the same plane; the front spar instead was fixed to a mobile support that could be raised by 1° 45' and lowered by 5° 30' by means of a screw system.

It was controlled by a mechanical device that was on the right of the pilot. The landing gear was retractable during the flight. It consisted of two equal and distinct semicarrellums arranged in the wings. Each was formed by a fork with an oil-pneumatic shock absorber, a fork that carried a FAST type wheel equipped with brakes with Pirelli 600x216x200 tires.

Each shock absorber shaft was connected to a horizontal axis that rotated in appropriate bushings fixed in the wing side members. These semi-carriages were each operated by a hydraulic jack which caused the stem to rotate towards the inside of the aircraft and made it disappear in the wings leading edge and in the central part of the fuselage in special compartments which were closed by doors in part fixed to the shock absorber and partly to the fuselage.

The tail wheel was also concealable during the flight. It was composed of an oil - pneumatic shock absorber with a wheel equipped with SPIGA 260 x80 tires. The trolley was equipped with a double FAST compressed air brake applied to the wheel drums. This air was contained in a cylinder fitted with a filling valve and was the same cylinder that was used to start the engine.

The normal pressure of the cylinder was 2O kg. about. From the cylinder, a pipeline went to a reduction valve. Before the valve, a socket was provided for the pressure gauge indicating the air pressure in the cylinder itself. The wing was monoplane with a thick and biconvex profile, of a thickness and depth decreasing towards the extreme margin. It was divided into three parts, one central and two easily removable side panels. The construction was entirely in metal.

Two spars with superavional insoles and spiked sides in superavional slab, suitably perforated, and stiffened with internal frames in correspondence to the ribs and diagonally. The connection attachments fixed to the ends of the side members were hinged in high resistance steel and with pins having a taper of 2,255 on the diameter.

The ribs in the central part between the two side members were built with profiles of duralumin connected to each other with riveted plates. The first two ribs were special, being wider and stronger than the others.

The leading edge of the wing was removable from the cart to the end. It was fixed to the front spar with screws. Its construction was similar to the rest, ie ribs in duralumin with superavional cover. On the two side members there is the rotation axis of the trolley.

This axis was then mounted on the wing while the lifting jack was part of the central plane of the fuselage. The leading edge from the head of the wings to the axis of rotation of the cart carried the compartments for the concealment of this. The wings were equipped with hypersupporters that went from the fuselage to about half wing and from this to the end of the wings there were the ailerons. The construction of the ailerons was completely in metal, with ribs made of profiled duralumin connected to each other, like in the wings of the wings, by riveted plates. The side member was in a tube divided into three parts connected with steel joints, and the hinges were made of steel with ball bearings.

The cover was in canvas. The hypersupporters were also built in metal, ribs and edges in duraluminium, spars in steel tube. The coverage was instead of superavional. The controls of the ailerons and the empennages were all by means of pipes, eliminating cables and related adjustment needs. The control of the hypersupporters was independent of that of the ailerons and was connected to the oleo-dynamic circuit of the trolley. The maximum lowering of the hypersupporting wings was 45 °. The Piaggio propeller variation command was installed from the 25th aircraft onwards, since up until the 24th aircraft the ethic was Fiat type with constant revolutions. The command was electric. To mitigate the effect of the propeller torque, the left wing was larger than the right wing (170 mm); while having the same surface, the semials obviously had a different rope at the end.

The propulsion was entrusted to a Fiat A.74 RC.38 engine, a radial 14 cylinder double air-cooled star, capable of delivering a power of 870 hp (618 kW), combined with a triple metal propeller of pitch construction variable in flight. 87 octane petrol. Unlike the G.50, which adopted the same motorization, a rusticated cowling was used in correspondence of the rocker arms placed at the apex of the single heads, thus significantly reducing the frontal encumbrance to the advantage of visibility. The oil tank was located in the engine castle and had a capacity of 42 liters; the oil cooler was on the outer front surface of the engine hood.

The armament was entrusted to two 12.7 mm Breda-SAFAT machine guns, one with right hand power and one with left hand power, complete with cylinders for pneumatic rearming. They were arranged anteriorly fixed and parallel to the aircraft's centerline and fixed on longitudinal supports adjustable in height and laterally, which were attached to the ordered n. 0 and behind the fuselage.

Each of said supports carried an adjustable double-acting shock absorber to absorb the impact of the shot. Their direct shot passed through the propeller just above the engine hood. In the middle, between the two weapons, there are two cassette tapes with a maximum capacity of 370 strokes each, starting from the 13th aircraft; for the first 12 aircraft the maximum capacity was 310 shots each.

In the fighter-bomber version, the M.C.200CB, the auxiliary hooks for two bombs up to 160 kg or two auxiliary tanks of 150 liters each were present under the wings.
At the date of the armistice 52 units were in service, 33 of which are still efficient.

On-board instruments

The instruments installed on board the aircraft are:

In the center:

- 1 - compass
- 2 - turn indicators
- 3 - 8,000 meters altimeter
- 4 - speed indicator from km / h 560
- 5 - variometer

To the left:

- 6 - windscreen opening command
- 7 - compressor pressure gauge
- 8 - 3,000 rpm tachometer
- 9 - oil thermometer
- 11 - brake wing
- 12 - telepirometer
- 13 - telepirometer switch
- 14 - siren switch
- 15 - warning light
- 16 - 15 atmospheres oil pressure gauge
- 17 - petrol pressure gauge

To the right:

- 18 - 2nd speed indicator from km / h 560
- 19 - Allemano type trolley pump pressure gauge with 250 atmospheres

- 20 - Allemano type wheel accumulator gauge from 80 atmospheres
- 21 - machine-gun rearming
- 22 - "Knook-Out" type fire alarm
- 23 - electric and mechanical indicator, trolley and tail wheel
- 22
- 24 - trolley circuit switch
- 25 - warning light
- 26 - Fast type trolley brake pressure gauge with 10 atmospheres Allemano construction.
- 27 - clock.

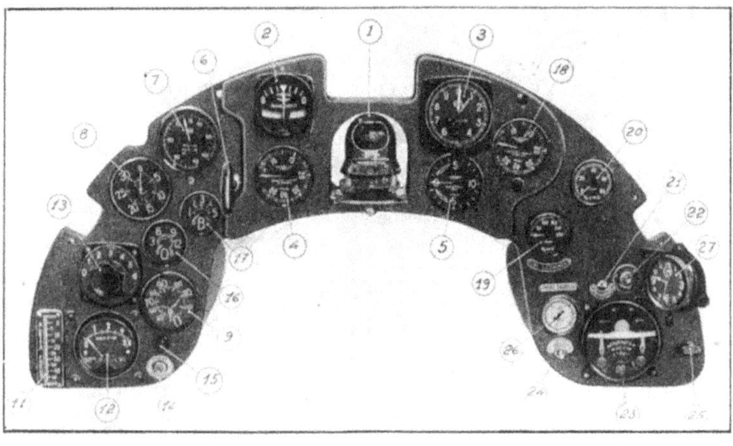

Technical features

Dimensions and weights

- Length: 8.19 meters
- Wingspan: 10.58 meters
- Height: 3.51 meters
- Wing area: 16,81 m^2
- Wing load: 142.2 kg / m^2
- Empty weight: 1,960 kg
- Load weight: 2,390 kg
- Specimens: 1,153

Propulsion

- Engine: a radial Fiat A.74 RC.38
- Power: 870 hp (618 kW)

Performance

- Maximum speed: 503 km / h at 4,500 meters
- Stall speed: 128 km / h
- Ascent speed:
  - to 1,000 meters in 1' and 3"
  - to 2,000 meters in 2' and 10"
  - at 3,000 meters in 3' and 24"
  - to 4,000 meters in 4' and 35"
  - to 5,000 meters in 5' and 52"
  - to 6,000 meters in 7' and 33"

- Take-off run: 260 meters
- Landing run: 300 meters

- Autonomy: 570 km or 870 km with two auxiliary tanks
- Tangency: 8,900 meters.

Armament

- Machine guns: 2 Breda/SAFAT 12.7 mm in fuselage synchronized and shooting through the propeller disk with 370 shots per weapon. The operation is recoil, with short recoil of barrel, and release of the obturator through the lever mechanism of Mascarucci. The firing cycle is closed shutter. The cooling is air, through the perforated cover. The belt feeding in the aeronautical systems was reversible, from the right or from the left.
On the fighters the machine gun was often used in a twin, fixed "hunting" installation on the engine hood, firing through the propeller disk. In this installation the shooting cadence dropped to 575 strokes/minute. Despite the 12.7 mm projectiles had low destructive capacity with only 0.8 grams of explosives and despite the availability of larger explosive high-caliber ammunition, Italian pilots appreciated the capabilities of this cartridge in the incendiary perforating version.

Use

The first M.C.200 were delivered to the Regia Aeronautica in 1939; on 10 June 1940, 144 specimens were in line, half ready for use, with the 6th Group of the 1st Wing in Sicily and the 152th Group of the 54th Wing in Vergiate. On November 1, the M.C.200 won their first victory, when a Sunderland on a reconnaissance mission was attacked just off Augusta in Sicily, by a patrol on a protective cruise. With the arrival, at the end of December, of the X Fliegerkorps in Sicily, the Macchi were assigned escort to the Junkers Ju 87 of the I/StG.1 and II/StG.2 in their missions on Malta.

At that time the German Stuka, in fact, did not yet have adequate protection, as the Messerschmitt Bf 109 of 7./JG 26 had not yet arrived. In combat with the Hawker Hurricane lenses, it proved to be effective, with exceptional performance in the air duels and without particular defects. From the entry into the war, in June 1940, until the September 8th surrender, the M.C.200 was the most used Italian fighter.

Operating in Greece, North Africa, Yugoslavia, the Mediterranean and Russia (where it obtained the excellent ratio of killing 88 enemy aircraft against 15 lost), the Saetta could compete with the best allied fighters, often coming out victorious. Before the end of 1941 the Spitfire was the only enemy fighter able to outclass the Macchi 200, even if the P-40 and the Hurricane of the advanced versions (especially if without anti-sand filters) could give big headaches. After that date, American top performance hunters began to progressively arrive, P-47, P-38, P-39, P-51, and in the same way the Soviets also replaced their old-fashioned devices with considerably more modern machines (in particular Yak 3 and Yak 9).

The British had progressively withdrawn the Gloster Gladiator and the Hurricane, replacing them (in 1941 in Malta and subsequently on all fronts) with Spitfire and Curtiss P-40, therefore, from 1941/1942 onwards the Saetta became progressively obsolete; the light armament did not allow it to act effectively as an interceptor. At the outbreak of hostilities against Yugoslavia, the Macchi of the 4th Stormo came into action. At dawn on April 6, 1941, hours before the official declaration of war, four M.C.200 of the 73rd Squadron took the first mission of this operational cycle, flying over the stronghold of Pula and pushing to the island of Cres, setting an oil tanker. The Macchi of the 4th Stormo rose in flight against Yugoslavia for the last time on April 14: 20 "Saette" of the 10th Group carried out an offensive cruise up to 100 km south of Karlovac, but they did not encounter enemy aircraft. Operations on the Yugoslav front ended on 17 April.

In eleven days the 4th Stormo lost no aircraft and destroyed 20 seaplanes on the ground, hitting another ten. In this period, all Fiat A.74 engines, produced under license by Reggiane, after an inspection by a captain of aeronautical engineering and a company engineer, were replaced for failures that brought oil temperatures to dangerous levels. For the Macchi M.C.200, the desert was the theater of major operations.

The first eleven M.C.200 arrived on April 19, 1941 at Castel Benito, those of the 374th Squadron at the helm of Capt. Favini. At the end of June only nine remained. On July 2nd, those of the 372^a, of the 153th Ace of Bastoni Group, followed on July 2nd. On December 8, 1941, the Macchi MC.200 of the 153th Group clashed with the Hurricanes of the 974th Squadron. During a fight, the British commander, Wing Commander Sidney Linnard, saw a Macchi attacking a Hurricane. Linnard tried to remove the Macchi from the tail of the British pilot, but the Macchi, veering closer, hit the Hawker's cockpit. The hit Hurricane capsized and swooped, killing the RAF ace (six shot down planes) of the RAF, Flight Lieutenant Owen Vincent Tracey. The July-December final of the 153th Group was 359 shares for a total of 4,686 hours and 54 opponents destroyed on the ground and in flight.

On July 20, 1942, the 18th Group of the 3rd Wing arrived in Tripoli with the 83ª, 85ª and 95ª squadrons. Twenty-one "Lightning", in all, fitted with two wingbill pillars weighing 3 kg, similar to the Fiat C.R.42 for loads up to 160 kg, even if four 15 kg were often hooked. The "Saetta", even as interceptors increasingly replaced by the more powerful Macchi M.C.202, also faced the first four-year allies.

On August 14, Second Vallauri second-wing Stormo attacked only four B-24 Liberators in the sky of Tobruk, succeeding in breaking down one. On 23 August 1942, three M.C.200 were launched on a Liberator group and the sergeant Zanarini and the second lieutenant Zuccarini shot down one. The budget of the unit, in that August, was of 198 aircraft employed in 394 hours on Tobruk, 1,482 hours of stock to 77 convoys. But the allied superiority became more and more overwhelming. In October the 200 Macchi lost from the 2nd Wing were ten. At the beginning of November 1942 the "Saetta" on the front line - between 2º and 3º Stormo - were only 15. Although outclassed in speed and armament by the latest versions of the Hawker Hurricane, the Curtiss P-40 and above all the Supermarine Spitfire, the Macchi could still get some victories.

In November, Lieutenant Savoia and Sergeant Major Baldi shot down two Bristol Beaufighter, while Sergeant Turchetti managed to shoot down two planes. But on December 1st, the 2nd Wing had only 42 "Lightning" in charge, of which 19 were efficient. On 29 March 1943, in the sector of Gabes, in North Africa, 15 M.C.200 intercepted P-40 and Spitfire declaring 4 victories at the price of a forced landing. Probably the first loss of a M.C.200 was recorded on Malta. On June 23, 1940, fourteen Macchi of the 6th Group, including nine of the 79th Squadron, eight of the 88th and one of the 81st, escorted ten SM.79 of the 11th Wing on the fortress-island. Two Gloster Gladiators were taken off. The N5519 piloted by Flight Lieutenant George Burges after attacking one of the Savoia Marchetti was in turn hired by the "Saetta" of the sergeant Major Molinelli of the 71st Squadron, off Sliema, in a "World War I style" air duel. Exceeded in maneuver despite the greater speed, the Saetta was hit and crashed into the sea. In September of the same year they flew to Malta to escort the S.M.79 bombers or the CANT Z.1007bis scouts.

On the morning of 25 July 1941 a Cant. A photographic reconnaissance of the 30th Wing was sent to Valletta to photograph the British "Substance" convoy that had docked the day before. About forty Macchi C.200 of the 54th Wing of Comiso and the 10th Group of Gerbini were tasked with escorting the reconnaissance.

About thirty Hurricane fell on the formation in Malta: the trimotore crashed into flames and two Macchi were shot down: that of the lieutenant Liberti, who died, and that of Lieutenant De Giorgi. The "Saetta" pilots declared the demolition of four Hurricane: two by the sergeant Major Magnaghi, one by the captain Gostini and one by the sergeant Omiccioli, of the 98th Squadron. Some specimens belonging to the «1st Stormo Caccia», belonging to the first production series, were withdrawn from the first line due to problems due to a faulty wing profile. Having corrected this drawback, the Macchi M.C.200 proved to be a reliable machine. Very manageable, he still had enough speed to compete with the Hawker Hurricane, compared to which he was superior in maneuvering combat, but exceeded as firepower.

The maneuverability and the robustness of the structure and of the radial engine were the only resources of the "Lightning" that - occasionally - and only thanks to the experience of the pilots could achieve some aerial victory. One of the last occurred a few days before the Armistice. On September 3, 1943, (or more likely, September 2, 1943) while he was patrolling the naval base of the port of La Spezia, Lieutenant Petrosellini of the 92th Squadron of the 8th Group was alerted by the fighter guide.

A flock of 24 American Boeing B-17 Flying Fortress was approaching. Petrosellini executed only two attacks, meeting the classic violent barrage of the B-17, succeeding in tearing down one and then carrying out an emergency landing on his airport in Sarzana. On 22 June 1941 the German offensive against Russia begins. Despite the sad experience of the Italian Air Corps in Belgium, the Head of the Government does not hesitate to offer Germany the sending of air units and, this time, also terrestrial. Thus, on 10 July 1941 the transfer of the Italian Shipping Corps into Russia (C.S.I.R.) begins. The initial aeronautical rate is formed by the 22nd hunting group (359a, 362a, 369a, 371a squadron) with 51 Macchi C. 200, and the 61st aerial observation group with 32 Caproni Ca. 311.

The aircraft arrive in Russia in the first half of August and advance from field to field, following the favorable fate of the land front. These territorial progress will eventually mark the fate of Italian-German forces lost in a desert, no less fearful than the African one.

Tudora, Krivoi Rog and, after the favorable operations on the Dnieper in late September 1941, Saporoshje. On November 9th, the 371th squadron is still further ahead, in Stalino. Despite some progress of the Russian counter-

offensive in December, the Italian-German troops remain in the Don area, until July 1942. What was this first Russian winter for the departments of our aviation and in particular for the departments of C. 200, is well illustrated by a page of the diary of the 371th squadron, compiled on December 6, 1941 by the captain Enrico Meille on the airport of Stalino: insufficient covering sheets, insufficient the same stoves and hot air conveyors; freezing of the pipes for the emission of petrol for low-speed operation; need to preheat starter motors and, much longer, engine oil; freezing in the hydraulic pumps control pump; freezing of the oil in the hydraulic circuit of the trolley with consequent impossibility of retraction, once in flight; specialists at work with 30° below zero, subject to frostbite on the limbs and face; pilots who find, in the open habitats, even lower temperatures and for which the same electrically heated overalls are insufficient, with consequent freezing phenomena; aircraft windscreens, reflecting collimators for shooting, the same glasses as the pilots, permanently tarnished with reduction to very modest visibility. Despite all this, when our fighters are able to intervene, they get good results on Russian aircraft. Between December 25 and 29, 12 Soviet aircraft were shot down against the loss of only one C. 200. On December 28th, the Italians were rich with successes: they shot down nine Soviet machines, including six Polikarpov I-16 fighters, in the area of Timofeyevka and Polskaya without losses. All these victories were obtained by the 359th Squadron. The 22nd Group - like the other units of the Regia Aeronautica - did not recognize individual victories. On December 29, 1941, the 369th Squadron lost the commander, the twenty-nine-year-old captain Giorgio Jannicelli, who fought a solitary air battle against more than ten I-16s and Mikoyan-Gurevich MiG-3.
He was awarded the posthumous Gold Medal.

On 4 and 5 February brilliant operations were carried out on the Russian airport of Kranyi Liman with the destruction of 10 enemy aircraft on the ground and the abatement of another 5, which rose on alert. Four other Russian aircraft were shot down in the clashes on 24 and 28 February, 14 during the month of March, 5 in May, 5 in June, 11 in July. In May, 10 more C. 200 arrived and in June, the staff of a squadron. After Stalino, the C. 200 pass on the airports of Borvenkovo, Makejevka, Tazinskaja, Voroscilovgrad, Oblivskaja, Millerovo, Kantemirovka: therefore always further and further from the sources of supplì.

Despite having to consider the now overtaken aircraft, it is in front of decidedly mediocre planes and not very well trained pilots. The loss of 15 Macchi C. 200, against 88 Russian aircraft, is proof of this throughout the campaign. But the real enemies of this unhappy expedition are the distances, the icy winter temperatures, or those other seasonal periods that bog down the airports and the communication routes, making it impossible to send supplies. The great Russian offensive begins on December 11, 1942. There are 32 Macchi C. 200 and 11 C. 202 in line, arriving at the front in September.

A fighter squadron abandons the advanced field of Kantemirovka in a hurry, while the Russians advance with imposing armored forces. The fighters, the BR. 20 and Ca. 311, the SMs. 81 of transport, they do in this very difficult period of full winter, what can be done: in just over a month, 27 among pilots, observers and crew, are deceased or missing. On January 17, 1943, the 21st group, which from the spring of 1942 took over the 22nd C. 200, framing them in the 256th, 382th and 386th squadron, carries out a last machine-gun mission in the Millerovo area with the use of 25 devices .

After that, all that remains is to fall back, trying to save the airplanes and all the logistic material that can be recovered. On May 15, 1943, the last aircraft leave the area of Odessa permanently to return to Italy. Memories tied to 1,000 km remain behind. advanced, the dispersion of a material that would have been much more profitable on the faltering African front, and above all the sacrifice of many soldiers belonging to ten divisions of the Italian army.

In Italy there were 30 Macchi M.C.200 and nine M.C.202, while 15 unserviceable planes were abandoned during the retreat. A total of 66 Italian aircraft had been lost on the eastern front for various causes, compared - according to official data - the slaughter of 88 enemy aircraft, during 17 months of action in that theater of war. Compendium of the operations: 2,557 offensive penetration flights, 511 in tactical support with the release of bombs, 1,310 machine-guns, 1,938 stocks, 88 destroyed adversaries; the 362[a] Squadron of Captain Germano La Ferla, who destroyed 13 Soviet aircraft on the ground, knocked down 30. The sturdy metal structure and the air-cooled stellar engine made it an excellent ground attack aircraft, often used as a bomber fighter.

22nd Group

The 22nd Autonomous Fighter Terrestrial Group, or simply the 22nd Group Fighter, was a group of the Regia Aeronautica that fought on the Russian front during the Second World War. The 22nd Group was sent to the front in the summer of 1941 with four squadrons formed by veteran pilots, the 359ª, 362ª, 369ª and the 371ª. The Group remained at the front until May 1942, when it was replaced by the 21st Autonomous Fighter Terrestrial Group. Starting from 1953, the 22nd Group was annexed to the 51st Wing of the re-established Aeronautica Militare of the Italian Republic. The Italian Air Force Corps Command in Russia was officially established on July 29, 1941 at Tudora airport. The Group landed at this airport on 12 August. The appliances were 51 Macchi MC200s that adopted a Mediterranean camouflage: a light ocher background, with a dense network of irregular green opaque stains, while the engine cowling, the band on the fuselage just behind the cockpit and the lower edge at the wing end were yellow.
On the leading edge of the wings appeared two large white triangles, with the point facing the inside of the wing. The identification and squadron numbers were painted black.
The Macchi were accompanied by two Savoia-Marchetti S.M.81 and three Caproni Ca.133 for logistical support. The 61st Air Observation Group with 32 Caproni Ca.311 (34th, 119th, and 128th squadron) and a Savoia-Marchetti S.M.82 for support arrived on August 16th. The emblem of the Group was a scarecrow on a white triangle. On the 27th of August, the Group baptized the fire, knocking down eight Soviet planes, two Polikarpov I-16s and six Tupolev SB-2s, without reporting losses. In the following

days the Soviets no longer took their devices, too old to the comparison of the Macchi.

The Italians therefore thought they had frightened the enemy, hence the adoption of the scarecrow smoking enemy planes, represented by eight red stars. The 22nd Group returned to Italy on May 4, 1942, leaving the aircraft to the incoming 21st Group. At the end of June, it will be risky in Sardinia with the new Reggiane Re.2001 and then in Sicily, under the command of Major Vittorio Minguzzi.

Then the department will go to the defense of Naples. Starting from spring 1943 one of the squadrons of the group, the 362ª, will be in charge of some brand new

Reggiane Re.2005 of pre-series, which will use in interception missions together with Macchi M.C. 202, to the Reggiane Re. 2001 and to the Dewoitine D.520 already in charge.

The first pilot to bring the new fighter into combat will be the commander of the major group Minguzzi. After the war, the 22nd Group, renamed the Interceptors Group, was integrated into the 51st Wing and operated with F-104S interceptors and, from 1989, F-104ASA. In 1995 he received the silver and bronze medal for military valor for his activity during the second world war.

On 25 February 1999, as part of the measures aimed at the reorganization of the Italian Air Force, the group was placed in "square position" and the last aircraft and part of the personnel were inherited by the XX Group of the 4th Wing.

21st Group

The 21st Autonomous Fighter Terrestrial Group, or simply 21st Group Fighter, was a group of the Regia Aeronautica that fought on the Russian front and on the Italian front during the Second World War.

Angry wasp symbol of the 21st Group

On May 4, 1942, the 21st Group (composed of 356a, 382a, 361a and 386a squadron) approached the 22nd Group, while the 71st Air Observation Group on Caproni Ca.311, consisting of the 38th and 116th Squadron, replaced the 61st Group. The groups were framed in the newly constituted 8th Italian Army in Russia (ARM.I.R.) strong of about 227,000 men under the command of General Italo

Gariboldi. The 21st Group, commanded by Major Ettore Foschini, was equipped with 18 new Macchi C.200. During the second battle for Kharkov (12-30 May), the Italians carried out numerous accompanying flights for the German bombers. In the month of May, the pilots of the 21st Group received praise from the commander of the 17th German Army, especially for their bold and effective attacks in the Slavyansk area.

During the German advance, in the summer of 1942, the 21st Group was transferred to Makeyevka and subsequently to Voroshilovgrad and Oblivskaya. Increasingly, the Macchi had the task of escorting German aircraft and on 25 and 26 July 1942, five C.200 were lost in air combat. Starting from the late spring of 1943, the Group is involved in Italy and will be involved in the air operations to contrast the disembarkation in Sicily. Following the events of 8 September 1943, the group will be dissolved.

Versions

C.200

Two prototypes (MM.336/MM.337) with Fiat A.74 RC.38 engine, closed cockpit, trolley and tail wheel fully retractable. First flight on December 24, 1937 in the hands of the test driver Giuseppe Burei.

C.200

First version of large series, equipped with modified wing profile and Fiat A.74 RC.38 engine. Starting from the 241th exemplar, the cab was completely closed and, after the first 146 units, retractable from the rear wheel.

C.200 A2

Factory designation of the version with Fiat A.74 RC.38 engine, and wing and cart of C.202.

C.200 B2

Factory designation of the version with Fiat A.74 RC.38 engine, and only the leading edge of the C.202.

C.200 AS

Version obtained by conversion of the specimens destined to the operational theater of North Africa Italian (A.S.I.). He fitted an anti-sand filter to the carburetor air intake.

C.200 CB

Version obtained by conversion of the specimens destined to the operational theater of North Africa Italian (A.S.I.) destined to the role of fighter-bomber.
They mounted two wingbars with 3 kg weightbars and the ability to transport a bomb of 50, 100 or 160 kg.

C.200 Bis

Factory designation for a specimen made by Breda, on the cell of the specimen MM.8191, equipped with a Piaggio PXI RC45 Piaggio engine capable of 1,180 hp (880 kW) at 4,500 meters (14,800 feet). First flight on 11 April 1942 from Milan-Bresso driven by Luigi Acerbi. The plane was then equipped with a larger propeller and a revised engine bonnet. The maximum speed in the studies was 535 kmh. It did not go into production as C.200 as it was replaced by more advanced models.

C.201

Prior to the C.200 Bis it had flown a C.200 (MM 436) with a revised fuselage and a 870 hp Isotta Fraschini-Astro A.140RC.40 engine. It was then equipped with a 840 hp Fiat A.74 RC.38 engine, instead of the 1,000 hp Fiat A.76 RC.40 not available. The prototype C.201 flew for the first time in August 1940 in the hands of the test driver Guido Carestiato, reaching a speed of 512 km/h, compared to 505 on average achieved by the standard specimens. In fact, the aircraft used aerodynamic improvements such as the fuselage without the hump back and the closed cockpit.

Fiat A.74 RC.38

The Fiat A.74 RC.38 Ciclone was an air-cooled 14-cylinder radial double-star radial engine produced by the Italian company Fiat Aviazione in the 1930s and mounted on numerous Regia Aeronautica airplanes during the Second World War, including the hunting monoplane Macchi MC200 "Lightning" and Fiat G.50 and the biplane Fiat CR42.

The Fiat A.74 was designed in 1935 by the engineer Tranquillo Zerbi and Professor Antonio Fessia specifically for use on fighter aircraft. The engine was an evolution of the US R-1535 double-star 14-cylinder, of which Fiat had acquired the construction license. Among the two engines, however, there were numerous design differences, among others in bore and stroke, and construction measures.

These were due to both the need to simplify production and to use self-sufficient materials. Moreover the A.74 was characterized by the adoption of a centrifugal compressor optimized for the 3,800 meters of altitude and by the transmission of the motion to the propeller interposed by a speed reducer.

The Fiat A.74 RC.38 represented a turning point in the production of aeronautical engines of the Italian company, until then set on 12-cylinder V engines. It was the progenitor of a series of developments designed to produce engines with displacement and consequent power expressed more and more, such as A.76, A.80 and A.82.

Although it is easy to argue that the Fiat A.74, also good at its appearance, remained in use, especially on the front line fighter, when its performance was already outdated, the engine was appreciated by pilots and mechanics for its excellent reliability (even when fueled with poor quality fuels and in difficult climates, such as in the Libyan desert or in the Russian winter) and ease of maintenance.

Technical features

- Manufacturer: Fiat Aviazione
- Number of cylinders: double-star radial engine, 14 cylinders
- Cooling: air
- Power supply: Zenith single-body carburettor with pressure limiter and pre-heating of the fuel mixture.
- Distribution: OHV 2 valves per cylinder
- Length: 1,045 mm
- Diameter: 1,200 mm
- Displacement: 31,250 liters
- Bore: 140 mm
- Stroke: 145 mm
- Compression ratio: 6.7: 1
- Weight: 590 kg

- Power: 870 hp (648 kW) at 2,500 take-offs
- Fuel: 87 octane petrol

Lieutenant Costantino Petrosellini

Costantino Petrosellini, born in 1921 was a second assistant pilot when he was assigned to the 41st Squadron of the 63rd Group, based on the Campoformido airport in Udine. Piloting a biplane reconnaissance Ro.37 completes his first war missions against Yugoslavia. In July 1941 he began training on the Macchi M.C.200 and was assigned to the 92th Squadron of the 8th Group. During his career, he is decorated with 3 silver medals for military valor and a Cross of War, in addition to obtaining a promotion for war merits, knocking down 5 enemy planes, including a flying Fortress. After the war he continued to fly in the Air Force, entering the experimental department. After leaving the Air Force, he continued to fly to Alitalia as the first Commander. He died in Rome on 21 January 2015. Below is an excerpt from the diary of Lieutenant Costantino Petrosellini, pilot of the Regia Aeronautica, during the period in which he fought in North Africa. I arrived at the 8th hunting group, in Benghazi (airport K-3) in early May. It had been a transfer-transport apparatus from Caselle (Turin). I was in command of a patrol of three Macchi 200, which also included Pisano. The formation of twelve airplanes was at the orders of the then Captain Veronesi (called "the Madonna of Loreto" for his ineffable qualities of character). I came from the 1941 operational cycle in Yugoslavia and therefore the difference in the environment was immediately noticeable. In Benghazi, in May 1942, we had cruise protection duties on the high-altitude port. Bacich had been in charge of the group for a few days, succeeding La Carruba.

The three squadrons were commander from Zannier (92a), Marcovich (93a) and Cecchet (94a). During one of the

protection cruises on Benghazi for reasons still unknown (perhaps a failure to the oxygen plant) the Lieutenant Franciosi crashed into the harbor. But the main purpose of that stop in Benghazi (after the brief advance by Agedabia) was the preparation of the group for the next offensive that Rommel was preparing. The K-3 airport was located on Balbia, just south of Benghazi. The Macchi 200 were lined up under the trees to save them from adversary observation. The general conditions were acceptable and we began to make the first experiences of radio connection. One day Serotini, who was on duty at the transmitter on the ground (we had only the receiver on board) told me (I was flying at a relatively low altitude):
"If you hear me, make a tonneau" and I did it.
"If you hear me, turn left" and I would veer.
Then he also told me "If you hear me, jump with the parachute" and I pretended not to hear ...
On May 22nd, the three squadrons of the group moved to Martuba 5. Martuba was a place in the desert, about 50 km south of Derna: a desolate place, without a blade of grass, with the sun on its peak, as in the movies.
There were five airports, populated by the flocks 1st, 4th and 2nd (ours), in addition to the Cr. 42 and Stuka of the 5th and 50th and the Messerschmitt and Ju 88 Germans. All ready for the offensive. As soon as they landed, in the morning, at Martuba 5, the dust that we already had on the head of the English reconnaissance had not gone away. And a few hours later, the bombers. It must have been three o'clock in the afternoon. A dozen Douglas Boston showed up, escorted by a dozen P-40s. They dropped at random, but the 1st flock took off en masse and were all shot down, except for a P-40. The night they made us a bombardment of retaliation on the camps, just finished up. The tents were still on bet and the English Wellington, one at a time, down flares and bombs all night long, to drive us

crazy. In saltoni, I found a hole (the shelters around the tents had not had time to build them), I put myself inside, in the company of a dead Pole (I noticed it at dawn) unearthed by the hyenas. The actual offensive began at the dawn of May 24, 1942, when the 4th flock attacked the entire English hunting force of Spitfire and P-40 on Gambut airport, and destroyed it almost completely. The surprise was such that they found the planes still with the "capotes" on the engines. The domain of the sky was ours, so we started the ground attacks in support of the ground troops that, from the line that faced Ain el Gazala, began the advance to invest Tobruk.

They were terrible and beautiful days: in the midst of the dust, the sand, the formations took off, attacked the targets (chariots, autocolonne, enemy lines, still and moving), landed, yes supplied, left, and so from dawn to dusk. My followers were normally Moressi and Pisano, but I also often had Monti, Pavan and others with me. Zannier had left the command of the 92nd, which had been assumed by Samson.

This frenetic activity lasted practically a month, until the fall of Tobruk (June 21st). It was a glorious period, interwoven with episodes of audacity and dedication that would be too long to enumerate. All or almost all the aircraft returned from the affected actions. Some, unfortunately, did not belong at all. We had very painful losses: Marcovich and Bottazzi, among others, were taken prisoner. I commanded the training that followed that of Cecchet. I saw the Bottazzi plane catch fire and land without a cart in the middle of a cloud of dust and flames, while the anti-aircraft kept firing wildly.

I really thought that he had not done it: instead the British treated him very well and with a lot of humanity. June 14, flock action (60 airplanes) against the lines and Balbla between EI Mrassas and Tobruk. We lost Sozzi and

D'Agostini. D'Agostini, just promoted to captain, had taken the command of the 93rd, in place of Marcovich fallen prisoner: he landed unharmed with the cart on, among the crazy Australians after days and days of attacks from the sky. He was shot dead (his body was found, a few days later, when Tobruk had already fallen). The gold medal was decreed to his memory.

But even the living were not far behind. Palumbo with a calf full of splinters set off immediately for the action, with the blood that dripped. And so Pavan. And all this fighting against the thirst, the heat, the sand, the blinding sun; and against the terrible anti-aircraft in the stronghold of Tobruk that decimated us. Acroma, El Mrassas, Ain el Gazala, Mteifel el Ghebir, South Signals, Trlgh Capuzzo, Bir Hakeim, Tmimi are names we will not forget: they have remained in the heart and in the heart of us survivors like the hours of our lost youth (I had then 21 years). We were going to strafe downs, "sleeping in the sand", to see the opponent in the eye ...

The Macchi 200 worked miracles, and we strove to be no less than him. As I said, Tobruk fell on June 21st. 33,000 prisoners, 6,000 dead, full warehouses, food, petrol, vehicles, weapons and clothing to no end. The entire 8th English army practically destroyed. On June 24 we moved to Ain el Gazala, on the British airport abandoned a few hours ago. On 29 June, with Moressi and Pisano, I moved to Derna to carry out the protection cruise at the arrival of Mussolini who, as is well known, returned later without being able to enter Alexandria. We rested in Ain el Gazala. Sweet name: the source of the gazelles. In fact, there was not a drop of water.

A little peace, until 5 July. That day, following the columns that supported the remains of the 8th army, we moved to Abu Haggag, close to the lines of El Alamein. We landed under a terrible sandstorm and it was a coincidence that someone did not leave us the feathers. On July 12th we started again with the guns. The Egyptian desert was not substantially different from the Libyan desert, but over there, like the sword of fate, there was the terrible depression of Qattara. A Dantesque landscape, a steep ridge of 300 meters in height and beneath quicksand for a length of two or three hundred kilometers and a width of as many. The air below was unbearable and the engines did not want to "pull" when, when we were flying over the base of the ridge we would go looking for the British trucks. On the El Alamein line, the English anti-aircraft was organized and we still had painful losses.

Casadio, of the 94th, launched himself with the whole airplane against the armored car of an English column and broke with it, stopping the entire column that tried to circumvent one of our cornerstone. But the more the losses were, the more the friendship between the survivors became tenacious, intense, intimate. Other names of places were added to the memory: Fuca, Bir Khalda, Qattara Spring, Salt Spring, Qattara Boring Works, Gebel Kalabin. The front stopped at El Alamein a few months. The war of position relegated us to the convoys of motorized convoys that brought supplies along the coast, from Tobruk to Marsa Matruh. It was a terrible job, because of the fatigue, the monotony, the climate: it is possible to imagine what it meant to take off at one or two in the afternoon, from the Egyptian desert, and take a two-hour cruise at 500 meters, at the minimum of speed on motorbike.

The plane was burning, literally: we flew with shorts, bare-chested, with only the life jacket and gloves to not burn your hands. Our logistics ... worked as usual: no meat, fruit or fresh vegetables. Only biscuits and cans, so all wounded by avitaminosis. And no mineral water, which instead abounded in the rear. The 92nd and 93rd (now commanded by Bissoli) remained in Abu Hag-gag, while the 94th had moved to Sidi el Barrani, which over all served as a support for the stocks. It seemed a dark job: but there were beautiful episodes.

We often saved the motorcycles from the sudden attacks of the "Beaufighter", bringing them down. Lancia was in turn knocked down, landed in the desert and returned to Abu Haggag, with the compass in hand, at night, on foot; and the sentries did not shoot at him. At the end of September, Rommel attempted the offensive, which failed due to lack of fuel. The group of armored divisions remained blocked beyond the English lines, on the south side of El Alamein's lineup. So it was that on the night of September 24th, the 8th group, with isolated aircrafts, was sent to machine-gun in that area to keep the British (especially two Indian divisions) stopped while the Italian-Germans withdrew to their starting positions with fuel remedied God knows how and transported to run on the spot. It was an epic, desperate action.

The planes did not have artificial horizons, nor radionavigation means. The illumination of the on-board instruments was a way of speaking, and there was no means of defending oneself from the blinding flash of machine guns when firing.

No one had ever flown at night with the Macchi 200 (except for poor Ruffini: only once!) And the landing in the dark, in the desert, certainly did not present particular safety features. In short, we had no losses: and even today I can not say whether it was fortune or skill. Miracle, certainly, perhaps of the two things together. On October 15 we left Abu Haggag and retired to Bu Amud, near Tobruk. El Alamein's English offensive was near and easy to predict and it was vital to have a second row.

Bu Amud had a fair amount of logistical equipment, derived from what had been found in Tobruk, abandoned by the 8th army in June. We began to escort the convoys arriving, even at a considerable distance from the coast, at the limit of autonomy. On October 26 "beccai", with gregari Moressi and Pisano, a "Maryland" at low altitude, just outside the port. He defended himself like a lion. The combat moved into the heaps above and I found myself alone with him. With a burst I hit him in the right engine. He began to "flap his wings" as a sign of surrender, heading towards the coast. I got into training with him: it was then that the gunner from the turret sent me point-blank a burst that I missed for a hair.

I fired again, until I saw him fall like a torch. The retreat had taken a bad turn: on November 5th we were in Benghazi, back to K-3. Tobruk had been abandoned. We protected Benghazi as we could from the British bombers.

We made several fights, but those now had the first "Liberator". We moved to Nufilia, in the Gulf of Sirte, on November 15th and on the 21st at Marsa el Auegia.

There we began to attack the British columns with the wing bombs: the attacks had already been mounted in Abu Haggag by a team of armament technicians led by the then captain engineer Carlo Cao. We mistreated them, we "pure hunters". But they, the harsh bomb attacks, had put them all the same. And now they were good.

Every day the 8th group, now decimated in both men and vehicles, took off and plunged into the desert against the advancing British armored forces. They were actions without breath: down from 5,000 meters, in a vertical dive, between the anti-gunfire that was firing wildly, in the terrible furnace from which many did not return. And then, long-distance flights in the desert to bring a salute from above to our isolated garrisons and voted for the sacrifice. Moressi and I flew up to Marada, an oasis lost in the Sirte. Almost eight hundred kilometers of desert round-trip, beyond any imaginable autonomy of the Macchi 200. Then landing with five minutes of petrol: just to not break your neck just outside the airport.

And on December 1, the 8th group took the last action before repatriation. We managed to remedy five Macchi 200s in all. We loaded them with the two wing bombs and machine-gun tapes and we went off into a hot hell. We turned off the sea and dove into the English positions towards Agheila. Incredibly, the antiaircraft fired only at the last moment and stopped immediately after we had entered the route of escape after the release and the machine-gun fire. In fact, twelve "Spitfire" plunged into our heads. We were lower and slower than them. We accepted the desperate fight. A Spitfire and two Macchi 200 flamed up in flames.

Monti did not find him anymore; Calsolaro, seriously injured, reached the coast by swimming. Samson, Lancia and I were disappointed, embittered, sad for not being able to do more, perhaps with the guilt of not having sacrificed us with others. On December 10th, from Misurata now invested by the British, without more airplanes, the survivors of the 8th hunting group returned to Catania with a formation of S.82 sent to recover them. The facts and episodes that I have briefly described, the details that have happened to me but which represent those of all the others, have as their common denominator the absolute sense of duty, the spirit of sacrifice without limits. Mario Bacich was always in the lead, in the most risky actions, in the most exhausting ones, in moments of greater commitment. Each of us found in him, in his firmness of character (which was sometimes revealed in explosive forms) the strength necessary to overcome sacrifices, bitterness, hardships, pains, regrets and fears. Human fears, at the sight of the dearest dead friends: what if tomorrow touched me?

It did not touch me, because maybe another fell in my place: these few lines, these tears that streak my face, are for you, unknown pilot friend, who now fly forever, eternally young, in the pure sky of angels and heroes.

Lieutenant Costantino Petrosellini 8th Fighter Group

Macchi M.C. 202

The Macchi M.C.202 "Folgore" was the best Italian fighter plane fielded by the Regia Aeronautica in a significant number of specimens during the Second World War. The plane showed that Italy was certainly able to design and build high-class aircraft. The Macchi M.C.202 Folgore was a single-engine single-seater aircraft with low wings designed by the Italian Aeronautica Macchi and also produced by the Breda of Sesto S. Giovanni in 1941-1943.

Employed in the Second World War by the Regia Aeronautica, it retained its predecessor, the MC200, wings and tail but had a much more tapered and aerodynamic fuselage and above all was equipped with the most powerful German DB601A engine, later built under license from the 'Alfa Romeo as RA 1000 RC41-1 at the new plant in Pomigliano d'Arco, at the time being finalized. On 10 August 1940, the test pilot Guido Carestiato took off with the prototype and climbed to an altitude of 6,000 meters in less than 6 minutes, with a horizontal flight speed of 600 km/h. The high performance that the MC202 was capable of, as well as making it superior as a hunter to the Hawker Hurricane and the Curtiss P-40, made it an excellent interceptor: thanks to its speed of climb the MC202 was able to put in serious difficulty the allied bomber units operating in the skies of the Mediterranean. In order to accelerate the production of new equipment, the production was entrusted to three different companies: Macchi, Breda, and SAI-Ambrosini.

Between May 1941 and September 1943, the date of the Italian surrender, about 1,150 examples of this aircraft were manufactured, divided into fifteen series, each of which introduced changes and improvements with respect to the previous series: for example, the MC202 series VII was the first to introduce armored cab and two 7.7 mm wing guns in addition to the two 12.7 mm machine guns housed on the engine cover, already present in the previous series; the M.C.202 series XI, also called M.C.202CB (Bomber Hunting), was equipped with sub-bases that allowed to arm it with bombs or to mount auxiliary fuel tanks.

All the Folgore who fought on the North African front, known by the generic name of M.C.202AS (North Africa), were also provided with special filters against the desert sand. The Macchi MC 202 thunderbolt was the best fighter of the Regia Aeronautica during the Second World War, even though its armament was always insufficient compared to the robustness, power and excellent quality of flight with which it was equipped. In an attempt to remedy this deficiency, at the beginning of 1943 his successor, the Macchi MC 205 "Veltro" took service: the new plane was fitted with a Fiat Ra engine. 1050 RC-58, the Italian version of the Daimler-Benz DB-605, and replaced the wing guns with two 20mm Mauser MG151 / 20 cannons.

One of the most beautiful hunts of the Axis, the "Folgore" was also an efficient and deadly hunter.

A great admirer of Macchi M.C.202, the major Australian ace Clive Caldwell, argued that the Folgore would have been even better than the Messerschmitt Bf 109, if only he had been more armed. The fighter proved to have excellent characteristics of speed and maneuverability and was armed with two 12.7 mm machine guns, which could be added, on request and with reduction of the maximum speed and maneuverability, two 7.7 mm wing guns.

Another of its positive features was its extremely sturdy construction that allowed its pilots to be able to hurl themselves into very steep battles with their equipment.

History

The same Board of Evaluation of the Regia Aeronautica which was commissioned to evaluate the fighter aircraft of the so-called "first generation" (Macchi C.200, Fiat G.50, Reggiane Re.2000, Caproni Vizzola F.5), in its The final report of September 1939 stated that it was essential for the next generation to adopt liquid-cooled in-line engines so as to reduce the frontal section of the aircraft and increase its performance. Given the apparent inability of Italian industry to design a new generation of modern engines, in line, it was decided to focus again on engines produced under license, in particular the Daimler Benz DB 601, of which Alfa Romeo acquired the construction license in November 1939.

Engineer Mario Castoldi, designer of the Macchi C.200 and the famous racing airplanes of the Schneider Cup, modified his aircraft, mainly for the fuselage, to install the new engine. The result was a completely new aircraft that was taken to the air for the first time already in the summer of 1940. The prototype of the MC202 flew to Lonate Pozzolo on 10 August 1940 using the German 12-cylinder V-engine Daimler Benz DB 601 liquid cooled, driven by Guido Carestiato.

The new aircraft took advantage of the increased power available (1,175 hp), the improved aerodynamic finesse of the fuselage and a closed passenger compartment with a folding hood to the right. The increase in speed was remarkable because the C02 reached 596 km/h at 6,000 meters, a share that was able to reach in 6 minutes and 26 seconds, very good performance coupled with excellent maneuverability. Baptized 'Folgore', the new aircraft is warmly welcomed by the Ministry of Aeronautics; it is immediately ordered in series but an important production program under license is also started, which also involves Breda in Sesto S. Giovanni and the SAI Ambrosini in Passignano sul Trasimeno with distinct production lines. Eight months after the signing of the contract, the first M.C.202 as standard leaves the assembly line while the prototype is completing the assessment tests carried out first in Guidonia and then in Furbara with highly positive results.

On the flight characteristics of this airplane there is complete and unanimous consensus and also the reception at the departments is favorable.

The adoption of anti-sand filters on the air intake of the compressor for use in a desert environment is one of the few changes made on the Folgore throughout its career; another is the adoption of the blind glass on the windshield. Since May 1942, two 7.7 mm wing guns are mounted, for which the predisposition is standardized: but given the lack of effectiveness, it is preferable to do without them and very few specimens will actually be equipped with them.

The Macchi fighter armament undergoes only another variation on the M.M. 91974 in the spring 1943, of two 20mm Mauser guns in subalary gondolas; but the increase in weight and aerodynamic drag caused by this addition penalizes the aircraft too much and therefore this solution will be abandoned. The equipment of the 4th Wing (31 aircraft) begins in June and is completed in September: the first samples are in charge of the 97th Squadron of the 9th Group under the command of Captain Antonio Larsimont Pergameni who remains for a long time with his pilots and his specialists in Lonate Pozzolo for training and operational set-up involving, among other things, about 100 detailed changes, however without major problems; among other things, the use of high-octane anti-knockdown gasoline was first discussed.

Also the 17th Group of the 1st Wing is equipped with the new Macchi fighters and at Caselle Torinese the machines destined for the 8th Group of the 2nd Wing arrive, but these, with great disappointment of the pilots, are immediately diverted to the 1st Wing at Campoformido (17th Group).

The baptism of fire in North Africa is the work of the 9th Group of the 4th Stormo (26 November), but the first fight ever took place in the Sicily channel on 30 September; the second lieutenant Jacopo Frigerio of the 96th Squadron is attributed to the slaughter of a Hurricane. The 9th Group is deployed in Martuba with only two squadrons left behind. The first fight between ten Folgore and a large formation of Hurricane and Curtiss P-40 is resolved in our favor with the slaughter of at least eight enemy planes. Finally, the Regia Aeronautica fighters are starting to fly with a car that, at least in terms of performance, is comparable to its opponents. In combat, the Folgore would have even outclassed the best English fighters on our fronts in 1941, the Hurricane, the Fulmar of the aircraft carriers and even the P-40s.

Even the armament, often considered their weak point, is revealed in the first period to the height of the British machines: they count on eight 7.7 mm machine guns, but the lower caliber reduces its destructive and thrown capacity. For the Italo-German aviation the battle of El Alamein begins October 9, 1942; on that day the RAF carried out over 500 sorties with violent bombing and numerous ground attacks on the advanced airports of the El Daba and Fuka areas, rendered almost unusable by the recent rains; at the end of the day the British claim to have destroyed at least 50 aircraft on the ground, while their losses amounted to 38 airplanes, 10 of which were shot down by Italian fighter.

Another mass attack on day 20, mainly directed against Abu Hagag and Fuka, respectively locations of the 3rd and 4th Stormo: the Italians and the Germans shoot down 11 aircraft but they lose as many, plus two planes destroyed and twenty damaged on the ground. After a pause of relative calm the British offensive resumes on the 22nd with attacks on the fields of Fuka, Abu Nimeir, Abu Hagag and another 27 fights continue until October 31st. Our hunting groups inflict significant losses.

Finally, in early December, the only 9th Group of the 4th goes to the defense of the port of Tobruk and after the fall of the city only the 202 of the 3rd Wing remain in Africa. The Folgore of the department are posted at that time on other fields with a section of the 18th Group at En Nofilia then at Uadi Tamet and the 70th Squadron at Castel Benito to operate in defense of Tripoli. After the fall of the city (23 January 1943) only C.202 of the 3rd Wing remain in Africa.

The effectiveness of the Macchi 202 on the African front was progressively consumed not by the machine itself but above all by the lack of personnel and by the scarce stocks of fuel and spare parts. From January to December 1942 the Italian hunting departments carry out a total of 23,555 sorties, 30% of which are attributable to Macchi M.C.202. With the Anglo-American disembarkation in Morocco and Algeria, at the beginning of November 1942 the 202 of the 53rd Autonomous Group and of the 17th Group (1st Wing), respectively 24 and 23, flow into Sardinia.

Together with the 2001 Kings, the Macchi fighters attack military targets in the areas of Bona and Bougie. In Tunisia, the 153th Group aircraft moved to El Alouina near Tunis; in February 1943 the Folgore departments in North Africa include the 6th Wing (79th and 81st squadron) in Sfax, the 3rd Wing in El Hamma and the 16th Group (54th Wing) on K34 and K41; in total there are 55 M.C.202 in Tunisia, spread over twelve squadrons. In this period the Folgore faces the first fights with the fighters of the 12th Air Force of the USAAF and in particular the Italian fighter must clash with the P-38 Lightning of the 1st and 14th Fighter Group, the P-39 Airacobra dell'81 ° and 351 ° Fighter Group and the Spitfire of the 31st and 54th Fighter Group.

On several occasions the 202 manages to cope with the deadly Lightning, due to its smaller turning radius, while it can also have the best on Airacobra. In any case, the poor armament of Italian hunting is evident. We recall the use of the Folgore in the Italian-German counteroffensive in Medenine which slowed the Anglo-American momentum for a while. In March the 202 support 21 fights during which they manage to shoot down several Spitfires, a P-40 and a P-38.

The last flight of the Macchi fighter before the armistice is the one supported by some planes of the 3rd Wing, under the command of Lieutenant Solaroli, who joins the one piloted by Adriano Mantelli, assigned to the command of a 51st Wing Group in Sardinia and passing through Foligno, took off on alert to intercept the B-24 that on September 8 carry out a heavy bombardment on Frascati. The M.C.202 built by Breda after the armistice are requirements and used by the Luftwaffe as advanced trainers and for the training of instructors in the schools of Orange in France and Garz in the Baltic Sea.

Others M.C.202 (at least twelve) are withdrawn by crews of the Croatian Legion at Sesto S. Giovanni at the beginning of 1944 and inserted into the 11th Squadron stationed at Kurilovek.

Technique

The cell of M.C.202 was different from that of M.C.200 for the shape of the fuselage, in the "Folgore" more tapered and without the famous "hunchback" of the "Saetta".
The fuselage was of the shell type of oval section.
The structure was entirely metallic, and consisted of four side members made of molded duraluminium plates and of duraluminium battens held by orderly also in printed duralumin sheet. The covering was in superaional nailed to the fuselage structures so as to form a very resistant assembly. On the front of the fuselage were the four connections for the engine castle. Two of these attacks, the upper ones, were on the ordinate in correspondence with the upper side members of the fuselage and the two lower ones on the longitudinal wing of the central plane of the wings. At the two ends of the longitudinal struts of the central plane were foreseen the interlocking attachments for the two half wings. Between the two side plates of the central floor was the main petrol tank.
Over the main tank were installed the machine guns, the boxes for the charges and the boxes to collect cartridge cases and sweaters. Two opening doors at the top of the fuselage allowed the maintenance of the weapons. The cockpit was again closed with the opening that happened by tilting the side of the roof, hinged on the right side, a procedure that recalls the system used on some gliders of the time. Immediately behind the cockpit were the additional fuel tank, the compressed air cylinder, the truck accumulator and the accumulator of the flaps. In the rear part of the fuselage there were the supports for the

receiver-transmitter unit, for the booster, for the modulator and the radiogoniometer.

The wing was cantilever monoplane, biconvex profile, of thickness and depth decreasing towards the outer edge and therefore did not cause those high-speed stalls which Macchi M.C.200 initially subjected. It was divided into three parts, one central and two easily removable sides.

The construction was entirely in metal. In the two semials, the left had an opening and a surface slightly higher than those of the right to compensate for the reaction torque of the propeller. The connection attachments, fixed to the ends of the side members, were hinged in high resistance steel; on the two side members there were the supports of the trolley rotation shaft. This shaft was then mounted in the wing, while the lifting jack was part of the central plane of the fuselage.

The ribs in the central part between the two side members were built with duralumin profiles connected to each other with riveted plates. The first two ribs were special, being wider and stronger than the others. The wing cover was in the superavional slab, bolted to the ribs and to the side members. The leading edge of the wing was removable from the cart to the end. The wings were equipped with hypersupporters that went from the fuselage to about half wing; they were made of metal, ribs and edges in duraluminium, spars in steel tube, the cover was instead of superavional. The construction of the ailerons was completely made of metal, with ribs made of a duralumin profile joined together as in the ribs of the wings by riveted plates. The longitudinal member is made of a tube divided into three parts connected with ball joints of steel. The cover is in canvas.

An FM-62 camera could be mounted at the root of the left wing. The empennages consisted of:

- A completely metal-made stabilizer made of: two high-strength tube side members, duralumin ribs, edge and edge in duralumin with wood filling, duralumin sheet covering. The incidence of the stabilizer was adjustable in flight.

- A balancer built in two halves that can be dismantled together. The main axis is made of steel tube on which the duralumin ribs are fixed.

- A drift entirely made of metal composed of: two high strength steel tube side members, duralumin ribs, front edge and duralumin lining. The depth rudder hinges were fixed on the rear side member.

- A metal steering rudder.

- A longitudinal trimmer placed to the left of the pilot against the side of the fuselage. It was composed of a flyer that carried a drum on which an endless cord was wrapped.

The cart had two legs (fitted with oil-pneumatic shock absorbers) retractable in the wing's belly with rotation inward. The tail wheel was fixed and sometimes partially faired.

The pilot seat, rather small in size, was ventilated, heated and equipped with an oxygen system and was equipped with an adjustable seat protected by a 44 kg shaped back armor and an anti-pillar protection pillar in the headrest fairing. The main fuel tank was in the fuselage (270 liters), between the flame-retarding bulkhead and the pilot's seat. Other tanks were in the central section of the wing, from 40 liters each and a reserve of 80 behind the seat of the pilot, all covered with self-sealing treatment. The tanks were made of duralumin plate, reinforced with internal diaphragms and were protected by a special coating against 12.7 mm caliber weapons. The oil tank had a capacity of 36 liters and was built in duralumin reinforced sheet internally with perforated diaphragms.

On the first copies of M.C.202, original DB 601A-1 twelve-cylinder V-injection engines with 1,175 hp were installed. The three-blade metal propeller with variable pitch in flight and constant speed was the Piaggio P1001, with a diameter of 3.05 meters. Cooling of the coolant was entrusted to a ventral ducted radiator at the height of the driver's seat, while the lubricant radiator was placed under the engine.

The supply of 419 German engines was exhausted, since 1941 were installed those assembled by Alfa Romeo of Pomigliano d'Arco with parts and components supplied by Germany. Later in 1942 the RA 1000 RC.41-1 entered into production. The electrical system also provided for the heating of the arms, the Venturi tube and the pitot tube, when the engine was started (also equipped with a crank-operated starter) and with the command (electromechanical) of the propeller pitch.

The Macchi M.C.202 armament was composed of two 12.7 mm Breda SAFAT machine guns (with 400 strokes) synchronized, one with right feed and the other with left feed complete with cylinders for pneumatic rearming. They were arranged at the front, fixed and parallel to the aircraft's centerline and attached to supports lying longitudinally and adjustable both vertically and horizontally.

These supports were attached to the ordinate 0 and on a crosspiece in correspondence to the ordinate 3. On each support was mounted a double-acting shock absorber and adjustable, to allow the recoil of the weapon. The weapon's throw was synchronized with the propeller's motion and passed just above the engine.

The 7.7 mm machine guns in the wings were mounted one on each side and were located in a special compartment between the ribs 7 and 8, just after the rotation axis of the carriage. The power was one on the right and one on the left.

Each weapon was equipped with 500 shots.

The firing knob carried the following written indications:
- "A" - firing of 7.7 mm wing guns.
- "C" - shot of 12.7 mm central weapons.
- "All" - I shoot all four machine guns.

The weapons could be collimated both laterally and vertically by means of appropriate registers.

Compared to previous radial engine firing, the Folgore had better ascent speed (rising to 6,000 meters in 5 minutes and 55 seconds) and was able to beat at over 900 km / h. The controls were light, well balanced and ready to respond. Despite the great power of their V12 engines, the MC202 did not yaw on one side in acceleration during take-off because, as for the MC200s, their left wings were 21 centimeters longer than the right ones: the longest wing generated more lift and so compensated for what would have been the normal tendency to yaw to the left.

The ability to compete with the Hurricane, the American-supplied P-40s and the Spitfire V in the first fights, on the Western Desert, was a surprise for the RAF pilots and became a formidable opponent thanks to the training of Italian pilots in the flight acrobatic. Many of the Italian fighter pilots encountered by the RAF and Commonwealth air forces were skilled and very experienced, having fought in the civil war in Spain; if attacked, even by preponderant forces, they did not avoid fighting, even in situations where the Germans would have preferred to get away quickly.

These tactics were not necessarily positive: the departments tended to wear out, the acrobatic training was emphasized too much with respect to combat tactics and target shooting, the flight formations were primitive, although some departments adopted autonomously the German two-pair flight discipline (called double routes, Schwarm, four fingers), in place of the single pair or of the trio. Moreover, the quantity of Italian aircraft (and Germans) in terms of flying steadily declined as production was still insufficient to cover the losses. In order to accelerate the production of the new appliances, the production was entrusted to three different companies: Macchi, Breda and the Italian Aerospace Company Ambrosini.

To respond, at least in part, to the expectations of a greater volume of fire by many Italian pilots, Macchi, starting from the IV series, installed two additional Breda-SAFAT machine guns, of 7.7 mm, in the wings. But these small-caliber weapons proved to be not very effective, so much so that many riders preferred to take them apart to reduce the weight in the wings even if only a few tens of kilos and be able to count on better handling.

The "Folgore" derived directly from the Macchi C. 205V "Veltro" that differed from 202 only for the adoption of the more powerful 1475 hp Daimler-Benz DB 605 engine, a larger diameter propeller and two tubular radiators for the oil, under the snout.

Alfa Romeo RA.1000 R.C.41 engine

On the first specimens of Macchi M.C.202 original DB 601A-1 engines were mounted. The supply of 419 German engines was exhausted, since 1941 the ones assembled by Alfa Romeo of Pomigliano d'Arco near Naples were installed with parts and components supplied by Germany. Then in 1942 the RA.1000 R.C.41 went into production, a four-stroke direct injection engine, 12 cylinders in an inverted V line with an angle of 60°, liquid cooled; the inverted V-shaped arrangement was preferred because it improved the visibility for the pilot, further removing the exhaust gas ducts from the passenger compartment. The cylinders are made of a steel bar inserted into an aluminum load-bearing block. The distribution system is based on four valves, regulated by rocker arms driven by a camshaft. Each cylinder has two spark plugs, powered by two magnets located at the rear of the engine.

A cylindrical gearbox is placed between the crankshaft and the propeller shaft. The power supply is supplied by a Ducati type fuel pump with FG3501 or Nardi 12 vane type gears, the second one with greater capacity. The injection is supplied with Iniex TPZ 12HM 100/11 or in the case of an inverted 12-cylinder Bosch PZ12 HM with automatic control that regulates the flow according to the pressure and temperature of the supply air, as well as the stop and deaerator device. commuter. The injectors are Iniex (corresponding to Bosch B94M10) or Orange 9-2029B. The compressor is a single-stage centrifugal equipped with a regulator, connected to a barometric capsule, which determines the pump flow rate: this is zero up to 2,100 meters and then progressively increases up to a maximum of about 7,000 meters. The maximum pressure is 1.45

kg/cm^2, allowed for no more than a minute while the recommended normal is 1.23 kg/cm^2. The ignition, controlled by a twin magnet Marelli MZM 12BR4 or Bosch ZM 12BR4 and using ceramic Marelli MR 405 or Bosch DW240 ET8 candles with ceramic insulation, takes place in the following order: 1/8/5/10/3/7/6/11/2/9/4/12.

Lubrication is guaranteed by a delivery pump and two double gear recovery pumps, while water cooling is served by a centrifugal pump that moves the water contained in the engine equal to 32 liters to which antifreeze agents and oil Shell or NP Nafta are added. equal to 1.5%. The serial production of the RA.1000 R.C. 41-1 began in 1942. At first the production was 30/40 engines a month and then rose to a standard of about 60/65. In any case, the problem of the insufficiency of this production remained open to the immediate need for the Macchi M.C.202 and the RE 2001 with consequent delays in the entry into line of these aircraft. Among the data obtained from the statistics of the Alfa Romeo we find that in 1943, about 1,750 fighter jets were delivered to about 1,750 engines, while the immediate necessity was at least 2,000 engines without counting the necessary reserves.

Technical features

- Dry motor weight complete with electric starter, with propeller shaft and R.A auxiliary controls. without exhaust pipes: 670 kg
- Length: 1,891 mm
- Width (excluding exhaust pipes) : 712 mm
- Height : 1,033 mm
- Displacement: 33.9 liters
- Bore: 150 mm
- Stroke: 160 mm
- Takeoff power: 1,175 hp at 2,500 rpm
- Power at 3,700 meters: 1,100 hp at 2,400 rpm
- Power at 4,500 meters: 1,000 hp at 2,400 rpm

Versions

Overall, 1,453 "Folgore" were ordered.
The bulk of the orders was:
- At Breda, 900 units, of which 649 products.
- L'Aermacchi itself, 403 units, of which 390 products.
- The SAI Ambrosini, 150 units, of which 67 products.

M.C.202 MM.445

The prototype presented a sort of "teardrop" roof, having two transparent ones fixed on each side on the rear fairing of the passenger compartment and the retractable tail wheel and closed by two small doors. the engine castle was not yet in light alloy, but in steel tubes. Instead, it did not have the air inlet on the left side of the engine bonnet, nor the radio antenna.

M.C.202

The initial serial version did not have the antenna wire support rod, which only appeared with radio transmitters. The first operational aircraft had, in fact, only one receiver.

M.C.202 AS

It was the "Folgore" "Northern Africa", equipped with a Corbetta sand filter at the air intake (applied to practically all the specimens). With the VII series the windshield was introduced in a glass-beam and the wing was set up to house two 7,7 mm machine guns with 500 rounds per weapon, mounted since May 1941. Because of the weight gain, however, which reduced the maneuverability , the pilots often took them apart.

M.C.202AS/CB

From the XI Series onwards, the Macchi M.C.202 could become AS/CB, ie Bomber-Hunting, with two wing attacks for bombs of 50, 100, or 160 kg, or 100 or 150 liter (rarely used) auxiliary tanks. The attacks were actually mounted on very few aircraft.

M.C.202EC

The Thunderbolt MM.91974 - tested on 12 May 1943 - was equipped with two sub-aircraft gondolas for 20 mm Mauser MG 151/20 aircraft guns with 200 rounds per weapon. Four other examples were made, but the Italian pilots, who had already rejected the 7.7-mm Breda-SAFATs in the wings, due to the weight increase, did not sufficiently appreciate the innovation.

M.C.204

Already in the autumn of 1940, in order to free itself from the deliveries of DB 601, a variant designed by Isotta Fraschini Asso L.121 engine or a derivative was designed. The construction of a wooden mock-up of the new face was made to define the installations, but the project was abandoned because it was realized that it would result in an unacceptable decline in performance.
Known simply as "C.202 Isotta Fraschini", after the realization of M.C.205, which took the last figure from the DB 605 engine, the project was later renamed M.C.204, to occupy the number remained free.

The name M.C.203 was instead assigned, again later, to a twin-engined seaplane on the preliminary drawings.

Technical features

Dimensions and weights

- Length: 8.85 meters
- Wingspan: 10.58 meters (left wing 21 cm longer, to compensate left yaw tendency due to propeller torque)
- Height: 3.04 meters
- Wing area: 16,80 m^2
- Alar load: 174.2 kg / m^2
- Empty weight: 2.350 kg
- Maximum takeoff weight: 2,930 kg
- Crew: 1
- Specimens: 1.106

Propulsion

- Engine: original inverted V-shaped twelve-cylinder DB 601A-1; subsequently (under license) Alfa Romeo 1000 RC41-1 Monsone
- Power:
  - 1,175 hp (864 kW) at take-off at 2,500 rpm
  - 1,100 hp at 3,700 meters at 2,400 rpm
  - 1,000 hp at 4,500 meters at 2,400 rpm

Performance

- Take-off meters: 253
- Landing meters: 235
- Autonomy: 765 km
- Tangency: 11,500 meters
- Maximum speed: 599 km/h at 5,600 meters

- Stall speed: 143 km/h
- Ascent speed:
  - to 1,000 meters - 0.39
  - at 2,000 meters - 1.28
  - at 3,000 meters - 2.28
  - at 4,000 meters - 3.32
  - at 5,000 meters - 4.40
  - to 6,000 meters - 5.55

Armament

- Machine guns: 2 Breda-SAFAT caliber 12.7 mm with 400 cartridges per weapon (from the IV series, two other caliber 7.7 mm wingers) with 500 cartridges per weapon.
- Bombs: Pylons in the CB version (fighter-bomber) with the possibility of installing two sub-aircraft beams for transporting bombs up to a maximum of 160 kg per beam.

Use

The Macchi 202 operated on all fronts.

The plane had its baptism of fire only at the end of September 1941, because of the many defects that the first specimens presented. Some could be eliminated in a short time. As the defect of the cart that - in some flights - after abrupt callback, came out. On 21 August in Lonate Pozzolo, Lieutenant Giulio Reiner, one of the most experienced pilots of the 9th Group, carried out the flight of military control and the instruments of the Technical Office recorded the spark speed of 1,078.27 km h and an acceleration in the recall of 5.8 G. However, during the dive some disadvantages occurred: the handwheel for the command of the tail plan was blocked and did not intervene in the recall maneuver of 202 which tended to remain in a candle.

Moreover, at the maximum speed reached there were very strong vibrations, particularly on the cloche.

Finally, the inclination of the propeller blades stopped at the maximum pitch even with the throttle at idle, facilitating the sunk but hindering the landing. Among other defects that could be eliminated, the bonnet of the splitting weapons, the tapes of the ammunitions that are jamming and the anti-sand air intake that, due to the vibrations of the engine, first crystallized and then sheared. Other defects such as the malfunctioning of the oxygen system and insufficient weaponry, could never be completely resolved. As well as the problem of radios, which emitted many and such noises that the pilots preferred to keep them off. The Folgore had its baptism of fire under the banner of the "Prancing Horse".

The first unit to record the first killing was the 9th Group (4th Stormo) on September 30, 1941.

On that day shortly after two in the afternoon, six Hurricane took off from Hal Far's base in Malta crashed into the Comiso airport, straining and throwing pieces.

Among the explosions, three Macchi of the 97th Squadron took off to intercept the British fighter-bombers. The lieutenant Jacopo Frigerio, having reached the British planes, bound for Malta, attacked the Hurricane (Z5265) of the Pilot Officer D.W Lintern, setting him on fire. The British pilot launched a parachute over the sea 15 km south of Cape Scaramia, north of Gozo. Shortly thereafter, a rescue Z.506 Cant escorted by three M.C.202 came to rescue the pilot, but seven Hurricane tried to break down the hydro-rescue.

The Folgore then attacked the Hurricane and several British aircraft were hit. Among these, one exploded before falling into the sea. On October 1, 1941, there was another fight between the Folgore and Hurricane of the 185th Fighter Squadron. About thirty miles north-east of the island of Malta, the British unit, the Squadron Leader F.B., was hit by burning the Hurricane IIc of the Commander. "Baby" Mold, a highly decorated pilot who launched himself with a parachute and ended up in the sea, but was never found again.

Also the M.C.202 of the 9th Group on November 26th 1941 met a Curtiss P-40 fighter formation and according to the Italian registers, broke down seven P-40s without losses. The presence of the Folgore in the sky of Malta only lasted until the end of November, when most of the Macchi was transferred to North Africa. The 4th Stormo returned to Sicily in April 1942 for a couple of weeks, before continuing his transfer to Campoformido. Meanwhile, the 16th Group of the 54th Wing began to re-equip itself with the M.C.202 towards the end of 1941.

The Macchi of the 51st Stormo and those of the 23rd Group of the 3rd Wing arrived in May 1942.

At the end of June, about 60 Macchi had been transferred to Sicily to operate against Malta, which had meanwhile begun to receive the Spitfire V.

Throughout the summer and part of autumn the Macchi collided almost daily with the Spitfire, with losses continue on both sides. On July 27, 1942, in the sky of Gozo there was a clash that featured the Canadian ace George Beurling (nicknamed "Buzz"), the 249th Squadron and the captain Furio Niclot Doglio of the 151st Squadron of the 51st Stormo Fighter, a skilled pilot Italian with seven accredited culls and many world records to his credit before the conflict.

Beurling on the Spitfire Mk V initials BR 301 / UFS blew up the Folgore (M.M.9042) by Niclot from a great distance. Before Doglio he also knocked down 202 of the sergeant Faliero Gelli of the 378th Squadron of the 155th Group, a pilot with three knockdowns to his credit.

Beurling, he used the "deflection shot", the distance shooting of fast moving targets and that same day also knocked down two Messerschmitt Bf 109, including that of Lieutenant Karl-Heinz Preu of Stabst./JG53, an ace with 8 knockdowns. He hit the Macchi of Sergeant Gelli even before being spotted and the same fate had to suffer also Niclot Doglio: intent to beat the wings and then maneuver and attack from the bottom other Spitfire, did not notice the side attack led from his left from training with flying the Canadian ace that hit it with several 20mm cannon shots.

"That poor devil just jumped into pieces," reported George Buzz Beurling, who for his achievements of that day earned the Distinguished Flying Medal. Two weeks later, on August 13, Adriano Visconti was sent on a mission to Malta to command an armed photographic M.C02 photo, paired with another Folgore in search of a fleet approaching the island. When it was on the vertical of the ships the two Macchi were attacked by four Spitfire escort to the convoy. Visconti, in his second fight with the M.C.202, knocked down two Spitfire, putting the other two to flight, allowing the scout to carry out his mission. For this double air victory, Visconti was awarded a Silver Medal for Military Valor. North Africa was the chessboard where they alternated more or less all the flocks that employed the Folgore, always available in insufficient number.

On the eve of Rommel's attack on Egypt that would take him to El Alamein, out of the 182 Italian ready-to-run fighters, 93 were Macchi 202. In October 1942, the 3rd Wing received the first Folgore and on the 20th of the same month, Lieutenant Franco Bordoni-Bisleri of the 83th Squadron of the 18th Group shot down a twin-engine Martin Baltimore of the 203 Squadron on Fuka.

Six days later, on the 26th, there was an air battle on Fuka, between nineteen Macchi 202 on one side and thirty P-40s and ten Spitfires escorted to eighteen Douglas DB-7 Boston on the other.

- Lt. Giulio Reiner of the 73rd Squadron hit a Spitfire that crashed and exploded on the ground, 20 km southeast of Fuka.
- Lt. Vittorio Squarcia, always of the same unit (73rd Squadron), in collaboration with other drivers of the 23rd Group, attacked a Curtiss P-40 and forced the pilot, Sergeant Emy Meredith, of 344 Squadron, to a retracted landing gear south of El Daba.
- Another P-40 hit by more Macchi crashed exploding on the ground.
- Bordoni-Bisleri hit one of the Kittyhawks, which was destroyed in a makeshift landing, 15 km southeast of Fuka.
- Only one Macchi did not return, that of Sergeant Major Celsus Zemella, forced to launch a parachute on El Quteifiya due to engine failure.

On 17 March, 17 Macchi M.C.202 fighter from the 16th flock shot down nine Spitfires and a Lockheed P-38, losing only two of their numbers. In the air the Anglo-American forces exceeded those of the Axis of 6 to 1, but also in this context Adriano Visconti, then in force at the 54th Stormo, on 8 April 1943 took off on alert together with the sergeants Giuseppe Marconcini and Domenico Laiolo. Visconti with altitude advantage and with the sun behind him led his men to attack a squadron of Spitfire V and took down the British commander. Sergeant Marconcini knocked down the left wingman of the British commander. Laiolo attacked a Spitfire that tried to escape reversing the course, but the Lightning anticipated him and hit him in full making him fall. For Visconti it was the fourth victory. On April 18th, between 5.25pm and 6.30pm, five Macchi M.C. 200 went to attack the tanks of the 1st Armored Division of the 8th British Army in Sidi Bou Ali. Twenty-two M.C.202 of the 54th flock of escort to the "Saette" collided with a formation of P-40 and Spitfire. Captain Sergio Maurer, Lieutenant Giuseppe Robetto and Sergeant Mauri shot down a Spitfire each, while Sergeant Rodoz precipitated a P-40.

Eleven days later, on April 29th, there was the last major airshow before the fall of Tunisia. In the morning, Lt. Oscar Patuelli of the 167th Squadron of the 54th Wing on a Folgore, surprised two enemy fighters taking off from an airport 8 km south of Medjez el Bab and knocked them down. On the same day, between 5.45 and 18.50, thirteen Macchi 202 of the 7th Protection Group to a naval convoy in navigation between Capo Bon and the island of Zembra, attacked sixty between Spitfire and P-40 directed against ships.

Lieutenant Visconti brought down a P-40 with wing bombs. Four others fell under the blows of other drivers of the 54th. Another five P-40s were declared probable. The pilots of the P-40s declared in turn three dejected Macchi, but the 54th reported only one loss, that of the captain Ugo Diappi of the 86th Squadron launched with the parachute plus the serious damage of three Macchi. Visconti was proposed for the award of a silver medal for military valor that will be granted on June 10, 1948, three years after his death. On the afternoon of Thursday, May 6, 1943, Macchi 202 of the 54th Wing rose to counter the dozens of Allied airplanes flying over Tunisia.

Visconti took off from Soliman at the head of the 7th Group, while Lieutenant Colonel Giovanni Zappetta took off from Korba in command of the 16th. The 14 Macchi

M.C.202 attacked in the sky of Capo Bon the Spitfire V of
the 31st Fighter group.

- Visconti hit a Spitfire (his sixth individual and final victory in the Regia Aeronautica) and probably a second.
- Another Spitfire was shot down by the pilots of the 7th Visconti Group and two others were declared "probable".
- Captain Sergio Mauer, commander of the 98th Squadron, was in turn shot down and almost certainly killed by Lieutenant Dale Shafer jr.
- Lieutenant Colonel Zappetta, hit by Major Frank Hill, was forced to make an emergency landing on a beach.

It was the last air combat of the Regia Aeronautica in Northern Africa: the day after Tunis surrendered to the Anglo-Americans.

In addition to North Africa, another front has represented for the Regia Aeronautica, a continuous haemorrhage of men and means: it is the employment against the island of Malta. A first presence of C.202 takes place in Sicily, on the Comiso airport, from 29 September to 24 November 1941 (9th group of the 4th flock). And it is precisely one of this theater that the aircraft achieves its first successes with the abatement of a Hurricane participant in the machine-gunning of the Sicilian airport of Comiso and two others of a formation of seven attacking the Italian hydrosoccorso sent to save the pilot of the first aircraft.

When these move to Africa, the Air Force of Sicily remains with only one section of C.202, equipped for photo shoots (Castelvetrano airport, beginning of 1942).

A more conspicuous use of C.202, takes place only in April 1942, when the 4th flock, returned from Africa and reinstated in Campoformido, stops in Sicily for a couple of weeks (airports of Sciacca and Castelvetrano). When in May the 4th flock returns to Libya, it replaces the C.202 of the 155th group (51st flock) and the 23rd group (3rd flock). In the sky of Malta, just on a C.202 of the 51st flock, on July 27, 1942 dies a valiant Squadron Commander: it is Furio Níclot, former world record holder of speed, on the Breda Ba.88. As of June 30, 1942, about 60 fighters C.202 can be used against the island. A new group, intended to operate against the island, must instead be sent to Africa urgently, and will never see employment in Malta. Meanwhile, the Roval Air Force line-up is kept constantly efficient, sending continuous reinforcements: 130 aircraft present on July 1, 55 to July 14, 112 to 23 July. At the last aerial offensive against Malta (October 1942), the 74 Macchi C.202 of three groups took part (in September, the 153rd autonomous group was added).

The 129 English fighters detected by the photographic surveys of October 10, on the island's airports, are reduced to 80, ten days later; but on 29 October, the launch of about forty Spitfires from the Furious aircraft carrier replaces the lost aircraft. All over again: but Regia Aeronautica and Luftwaffe no longer have the strength to start again; what little there is, it ends up in El Alamein. From June 1940 to November 1942, Malta's air defense nevertheless cost the RAF, 844 fighter aircraft (mostly Hurricane and Spitfire) and 518 pilots.

Parallel to the actions on Malta, it should be noted the contribution made by the departments of C.202, to the airship battles of "mid-June" and "mid-August" 1942.

Another front that saw the use of the aircraft, is the Russian. The Folgore arrived on the eastern front in the summer of 1942. The M.C.202 went to support or replace the Macchi 200 in force at the 21st Group. During the battle of the Don - the Italian fighters were then based on the airports of Millerovo and Kantamirovka - the aviators were engaged in combat and on August 13, seven Italian pilots were decorated with the second-class German cross. Subsequently, however, the 21st Group, which had 17 M.C.202 in force, employed the Folgore in a limited way: in the course of four months, the 202 only had 17 missions.

One of these was the escort to Junkers Ju 52 in flight on Stalingrad, December 11, 1942, during which the lieutenant pilot Gino Lionello was shot down and had to parachute from his Folgore. Five days later, on December 16, when the Soviets launched the offensive against the 8th Italian Army in Russia, or "ARMIR", the Macchi MC202 deployed on the eastern front were reduced to 11. Just two days later, under pressure of the Red Army and the Soviet aviation attacks, Kantamirovka airport had to be abandoned.

One of the "axes" of the Folgore was the "Spanish" veteran Franco Lucchini who added 21 culls to his 5 victories in Spain. Piloting the Macchi M.C. 202 obtained at least 16 individual victories and several others in collaboration on Libya, but was shot down and killed on Sicily on July 5, 1943. The Macchi 202 remained in the forefront even beyond the armistice. When the Regia Aeronautica resumed the war activity alongside the Allies, some Folgore equipped up to the complete wear of departments such as the 208th Fighter-Bomber Squadron.

In the north the few remaining devices were used for the training of the R.S.I. After the conflict, the Folgore no longer able to fly and not reconditioned in Macchi M.C. 205 to be sold abroad were used for years as targets for the training of firearms with the Breda-SAFAT 12.7 mm, until complete destruction.

Captain Franco Lucchini

Franco Lucchini, Captain of the Italian Air Force, was a war hero of the Second World War decorated with the gold medal for military memory. With 22 downs he was among the best aces of the Italian Air Force during the Spanish Civil War and the Second World War.

According to some sources, the war budget would amount to 26 individual airline victories (and a further 52 shared with other pilots), including the 5 abatements obtained in Spain. Franco Lucchini was born in Rome on December 24, 1917. His passion for flying was stimulated by the stories of two family friends such as Gian Giacomo Chiesa, director of the school of piloting Cerveteri, and Colonel Bertolini, commander of the airport of Furbara, then fell into the skies of Ethiopia. Lucchini joined the Regia Aeronautica as a complementary officer in 1935. He obtained the military pilot's license at the Air Force School of Foggia in July 1936 and was later assigned to the 91st Squadron of Hunting Airplanes of the 4th Wing.

In 1937 Lucchini decided to leave voluntary for the Spanish civil war. On 22 July he embarked in Ostia on a freighter heading for Cadiz. It was assigned to the 19th Squadron, 23rd Legionary Aviation Hunting Group, based in Torridoe and equipped with Fiat C.R.32 biplane fighters. During the Spanish civil conflict, Lucchini was credited with 5 air victories, in the course of 122 flight missions.

He was in turn knocked down twice, the second, on 22 July 1938, by the Polikarpov I-16 escort, after plunging a Tupolev ANT-40 bomber (Tupolev SB-2).

Launched with a parachute, he was taken prisoner but managed to escape in February 1939. His victories in

Spain earned him the promotion of the role of an actual role-playing officer and a Silver Medal for Military Valor. However, the number of its abatements in Spain is - according to some historians - overestimated, perhaps with the intention of making it appear, in front of the public opinion, as the "Second World War Barack". According to some sources, in fact, in Spain, Lucchini would have obtained only a confirmed victory, in addition to others in collaboration with other pilots. At the end of the civil war Lucchini returned to his original department to then go to the 90th Squadron of the same Stormo Caccia in April 1940. The 90th Squadron, after being reequipped with the new Fiat CR42 fighter, was sent to North Africa, where on 11 June 1940 Lucchini flew for the first war mission to protect Tripoli.

On 21 June, he attacked a Short Sunderland, already attacked without result by another Fiat C.R.42 and two C.R.32 off Tobruk. Lucchini hit the big English plane, leaving it with two engines that smoked. He did not claim the destruction but two days later, from the naval base of Bardia they announced that an airplane of that type had been found sunk, with heavy damage and only a surviving crew member, even if wounded. Despite being a victory by Lucchini, the killing was also attributed to the other three drivers.

In the great air battle of 4 August 1940 on the Ridotta Capuzzo, Lucchini, lieutenant of the 90th Squadron, brought down a Gloster Gladiator with 385 shots, near El Adem. It was most likely the one piloted by the Flight Lieutenant Marmaduke Pattle "Pat", destined to become one of the largest allied "axes", with about 50 shot down planes, and with the highest number of Italian aircraft shot down in World War II; of his blast he noticed as an exceptional shooter, able to calculate with great accuracy the trajectory of the bullets and that of the opponent's plane. During this first cycle of operations in North Africa, Lucchini was awarded 3 individual airline victories and 15 in collaboration, during 94 missions and 13 air fights.

He was decorated with a second Silver Medal for Military Valor and two Bronze Medals for Military Valor. At the beginning of 1941 the 90th Squadron was sent to Italy to be reequipped with the new Macchi M.C.200 fighters and subsequently, on June 16th 1941, in Trapani, Sicily to take part in the operations against the island of Malta.

On 27 June 1941 he broke down a Hawker Hurricane, and subsequently shared many other victories with his teammates. In September 1941, Lucchini was again decorated with a Silver Medal for Military Valor and, in December of the same year, he was appointed commander of the 84th Squadron. Shortly after the promotion, the unit was sent to Udine to be reequipped with the Macchi M.C.202 fighters.

On April 3, 1942, the 4th Stormo began to return to Sicily, where it was based in November and December 1941, with the arrival of the 10th Group, coming from Rome-Ciampino, to Castelvetrano. The unit, strong of 26 new Macchi M.C.202, was led by Lucchini, currently credited with the abatement of 14 enemy aircraft, plus one in collaboration. On 9 May Lucchini drove to Malta another 15 pilots on Macchi 202, escorted to five CANT Z. 1007bis. Thirty-three Spitfire attacked the formation.

The RAF declared the abatement of 3 bombers and a fighter. In reality, all Italian aircraft returned to base, with only a "Lightning" hit by a 20 mm bullet. Lucchini claimed a defeated Supermarine, but the RAF declared no losses. On May 22nd 1942 the entire 4th Wing, after having reequipped its fighters with tropicalized suction filters, was again sent to North Africa, near Martuba to participate in the Italian-German offensive by General Rommel against the British troops. On 4 June, Lucchini claimed the abatement of a P-40 in the skies of Bir Hacheim and on June 17 he knocked down another P-40 on Sidi Rezegh. On 10 July 1942, he led another 10 Macchi 202 of the 84th Squadron, before escorting to the C.R.42 of the 158th Group in the area of El Alamein, and then on a free hunting mission. Lucchini sighted a formation of 15 CurtissP-40 and brought his formation to the attack. The Curtiss formed a Lufbery defensive circle. After thirty minutes, exhausted the ammunition, the Macchi returned to the base.

Lucchini claimed the demolition of a P-40 (another seven were declared downed by the pilots of his formation and the 90th Squadron). On September 2, at 06:00, Lucchini is flying with another 17 Macchi of the 10th Group led by Major Giuseppe D'Agostinis on a free hunting mission.

They met two formations of 18 Douglas Boston and one of 12, escorted by thirty-five Spitfire on the Bir Mseilikh area. In the battle that followed Lucchini declared the demolition of a Boston and a Spitfire. Operators of the German radar Freya on October 20 delayed in identifying a large number of allied aircraft and Lucchini, with another 13 pilots of the 4th Stormo, intercepted 24 Boston and Lockheed Hudson still in action on Fuka, escorted by 30 P-40 and 20 Spitfire . Lucchini damaged a Hudson (the entire 4th Stormo claimed the downing of 24 enemy aircraft) but his M.C.202 was damaged by a 20 mm cannon shot and was forced to make an emergency landing.

On October 24, 1942, Lucchini was injured in the arm and legs during a flight mission. Immediately sent to the Fuka hospital he was then sent back to Italy for a period of convalescence. During this second round in Africa Lucchini deserved a second class Iron Cross conferred by the German allies for the courage shown in action. At the beginning of 1943 the Italian-German defeat in North

Africa led to the risk of the 4th Storm in Italy to try to counter any landing on the Sicilian coast by the Allied forces. Between the months of January and June the department was partially reequipped with the new Macchi M.C.205 fighters.

Lucchini returned to service in March 1943 and was promoted to the command of the 10th Group. On July 5, 1943 Lucchini, at the controls of a Macchi MC202, took off at 10:25, with another 26 MC202 and MC205 of the 4th Stormo to intercept 52 bombers escorted by dozens of Supermarine Spitfire fighters, aimed at bombarding the airports around Catania. Captain Lucchini commanded the 10th Group, formed by the 84th, the 90th and the 91st Squadron.

On the vertical of Gerbini, Lucchini, after having shot down an escort hunt (his 26th victory) attacked the formation of B-17, which he met for the first time. After having damaged several bombers Lucchini's hunt was seen to fall, with the roof closed, a few kilometers east of Catania. Lucchini's body was found two days later.

At his death, Lucchini had been decorated with five military-grade silver medals, a military-grade bronze medal, three military valor war crosses and a second-class German Iron Cross. He was quoted in the War Bulletin on September 5, 1942 and July 6, 1943. His victories had been obtained in 70 air fights during 262 combat missions.
In 1952 it was decorated to the memory with the Gold Medal to the posthumous Military Valor.
His body rests at the Air Force Memorial at the Verano cemetery, Rome.

Specimens

- Macchi C.202 "73-7 / M.M. 9667 (serial number 366)"

Currently on display at the Historical Museum of the Italian Air Force in Vigna di Valle, near Bracciano, this C.202 was built by Breda in early 1943 as a champion of the XI Series. In March 1943 he was assigned to the 54th Wing of the Royal Air Force and subsequently served in the 5th Wing, with the Cobelligerante Air Force. After the war it was used as a training aircraft at the Naval Academy of Livorno.
Currently the plane has the signs of the Giulio Reiner ace; unfortunately not all parts of the aircraft are original (a bonnet panel comes from a Macchi C.205 Veltro).

- Macchi C.202 "M.M. 9476"

Indicated as belonging to the 90th Squadron, 10th Group, 4th Wing, is depicted in the Gallery 205 above the diorama of the Second World War at the Smithsonian National Air and Space Museum in Washington.
The restoration was completed in the mid-1970s. No identification marking was found. It could be originally a VI or IX series, probably the M.M. 9476 prototype.

Macchi M.C. 205

The Macchi M.C.205V "Veltro" was an Italian single-engine propeller with a straight wing designed by Mario Castoldi and built by Aeronautica Macchi from the second half of the Second World War. Together with the Reggiane Re.2005 and the Fiat G.55, the Macchi M.C.205 was one of the three Italian "5 series" fighters designed to use the German engine Daimler-Benz DB 605.

The "Veltro" was a development of the Macchi M.C.202 "Folgore" and was used by the Regia Aeronautica since February 1943. He completed his activity with the Egyptian and Italian aeronautics at the beginning of the fifties.

Achieving a top speed of 642 km/h, equipped with a pair of 20 mm guns or with 2 Breda-SAFAT 12.7 mm machine guns, the Macchi MC205 "Veltro" was, according to some, among the best aircraft Italians from the Second World War. In combat he proved to be able to compete with enemy aircraft of the time, destroying several enemy bombers and easily coping with fighter planes such as the

North American P-51D Mustang, a capability that drove the Luftwaffe to use a number of these aircraft to equip your own Gruppe.

Although the M.C.205 was able to deal with the best opponents in terms of speed and maneuverability, it was introduced too late in the conflict to be of some impact on the air battle. Moreover, due to the scarce Italian industrial capacity, a limited number was produced before the end of hostilities.

The main axes of the Italian aviation achieved many of their victories with the M.C.205: Adriano Visconti, the greatest Italian ace, knocked down 11 of his 26 victories recognized with this airplane; Luigi Gorrini, knocking down 14 enemy planes and damaging another six, was the main ace of the "Veltro".

History

The Macchi M.C.205 Veltro, always designed by Ing. Castoldi, was essentially an evolution of the previous Macchi MC202 Folgore, obtained thanks to the installation, in the same cell, of a Fiat RA 1050 RC 58 Tifone engine, an Italian version built under license of the 1,475 hp Daimler-Benz DB 605, which it developed about 300 hp more than the Alfa Romeo RA.1000 RC.41 Monsoon (construction under license of the Daimler-Benz DB 601) used on the Folgore, and a more powerful armament.

The "kinship" between 202 and 205 was so close that at first the new version was not only called C202 Bis, but it was not even foreseen the realization of a real prototype, because we proceeded to modify a 202 of the IX series directly: the MM sample 9487. With the power taken from the 1,175 hp at the takeoff of the DB.601A to the 1,475 at the launch of the DB605A it was possible to increase the speed, the armament and reduce the climbing time, improvements without which it was impossible to fight on equal terms with the most modern hunting opponents. The Veltro was distinguished from the Folgore mainly by having the oil cooler split into two "barrel" elements rather than a single component and for a new propeller and its ogive. The splitting of the oil cooler was necessary to allow the flow of air to reach the coolant radiator placed behind it more easily.

The new ogive contained the Piaggio propeller pin and the more cumbersome reduction gear of the DB.605. The changes allowed to make the most of the engine power, but altered the particularly refined line of the Folgore. Hunting of the "5 series" (M.C.205, Fiat G.55 and Reggiane Re.2005) was the one produced in the most number of specimens.

In reality the real new hunting of the "5 series" of engineer Castoldi should have been the most advanced Macchi C.205N Orione (N should be for "Nuovo"), of which two prototypes were set up. The Regia Aeronautica, however, thought well to start the mass production of the Veltro, for which the assembly lines of the MC.202 could be used, and to forget the Orion, which would have required a long operation to modify the construction machinery. In a similar way to what was happening at the same time in Great Britain with Spitfire IX, the "temporary" derivative of the Spitfire V, the version conceived as an intermediate substituted the final one.

The numerical availability, given the production that produced about 181 specimens before September 1943 (128 within the first 7 months of the year), was halved at the time of the Armistice due to the losses suffered for accidents and for enemy actions. The production was resumed in the following October and finally suspended after the Macchi workshops were seriously damaged by the bombings of 30 April 1944. The Series II, 300 cars, had been assigned to the Fiat-Aeritalia, but due to the usual split and rivalry between the aeronautical industries, the precedence was given to G.55 which, although it was more modern, was late and it did not follow.

Compared to Bf 109 (and also to its competitors of the "5 series", the Fiat G. 55 and the Reggiane 2005) Macchi, however, had the "defect" of a "craft" design, which translated into longer times of processing. In fact, the work hours required to make the plane were around 20,000, about three times the BF 109G (but not very different from those needed to assemble a Spitfire). In practice, however, this defect, which the Macchi M.C.205V shared with its predecessor M.C.202 (to assemble which required 18,000 hours of work), never affected the production speed of the aircraft.

The factories of production of the "intermediate" and "5 series" fighters, in fact, always worked at a reduced pace compared to their possibilities, given the slowness of Alfa Romeo and Fiat in supplying them with the necessary engines and because of the always greater difficulty in finding strategic materials for aeronautical constructions: the production rate was about 12 "Veltro" per month, when it had succeeded in producing a three-times higher number of Macchi 202.

Overall the Macchi MC205V was an excellent aircraft: Luigi Gorrini, one of the best Italian aces of the war, with 19 accredited downs, even remarked his dowries with the engine off, when he managed to come back from the Volturno to Pratica di Mare , with the engine hit by bullets and seized by overheating.

"The 205 - recalls Gorrini - *was maneuverable as a bicycle.You could land in the wing slip as with the Fiat CR42.But also provided an excellent shooting platform, even more solid than the manufacturer had calculated. a perfect centering, which allowed to take off with the trim*

Like all the fighters that had a motor evolution during the war, the C.205V, suffered however the phenomenon of the increase of the wing load. As more and more powerful and heavy engines and armaments were installed on cells and, above all, wing plants, which were basically the same, the planes gained speed, but they lost agility and became easier to stall. On C.205V, which derived its wing plan from the light C.200, with respect to which it weighed, at full load, 50% more, the phenomenon caused a progressive loss of sensitivity of the aircraft at the controls of the pilot starting from 7,000 meters of altitude. For this reason the Macchi M.C.205V was selected by the Regia Aeronautica as interceptor from low and intermediate altitudes, while for the high altitude it was preferred the Fiat G.55, which had a completely redesigned cell and wings compared to its predecessor G.50.

In operational terms, the Italian pilots were very happy to have a car that was up to the times, which, due to its speed and firepower, allowed a leap in quality compared to the predecessors of the "intermediate series". As evidence of this fact we can report the company of Luigi Gorrini, who managed to shoot down three enemy planes, (two B-17s and a P-38, all confirmed, aimed at bombing a German division near Sulmona) already in its first mission with this plane.

In the last months before the armistice several prototypes were derived for high altitude hunting. Among these the most famous is the MC205N-1 Orione, which featured a wing of greater size (19 m²) and armed with a 20 mm cannon shooting in the propeller hub, as well as four 12.7 mm machine guns. , two in the semiali and two in the fuselage. The N-2 presented a different armament, with three 20 mm caliber aircraft guns (two instead of the machine guns of the wings) and two 12.7 mm caliber machine guns. However, the increase in the wing area with the same engine power was not without consequences on performance. The maximum speed indicated dropped from 642 to 629 km / h, while the time to rise to 8,000 meters had increased from about 9 to 10 minutes. The design phase of two new models with a larger wing area was also started:

- MC206: similar to the Orion but to be powered by the Daimler-Benz DB 603 with 1,750 hp, equipped with a wing surface increased to 21 m², speed 640/700 km / h, armament: 1st version 2 caliber machine guns 12.7 mm in fuselage and 3 20 mm diameter guns, one located in the propeller hub and the other two on the wings; 2nd version four wing guns 20 mm caliber.
- M.C.207: similar to the 206 in almost all aspects (the maximum weight passed however from 3.650

to 4.340 kg), it fitted the DB 603 from the beginning and the estimated speed rose to 700/740 km / h. The armament was four MG 151/20 caliber 20 mm guns in the wings.

But none of the two aircraft arrived at the complete construction of the prototype due to the deteriorated situation at all levels and the heavy Allied bombings that were mainly aimed at stopping the construction of the 205V.

In the last weeks of the war in the summer of 1943, twelve Veltro were transformed into scouting photos with the installation in the fuselage, behind the piloting station, of a German electric planimetric photo camera Riehenbildner RB50/30 with Zeiss lenses and film 30 x 30 cm.

The modification led to the landing of the radio system and its stylus antenna, of the rear tank of 80 liters, the opening of a hole in the bottom of the fuselage, concealable with a pilot control, and the assembly of a timer in the passenger compartment .

The conversion was carried out in Guidonia and also provided for the possibility of hooking two 100 or 150 liter tanks to the special sub-aircraft beams, in order to increase the range of action. The department that employed the RF version was the 110th Squadriglia JIO "Aero Photographic Squadron Fighter" commanded by the captain Adriano Visconti The squadron was established in Guidonia (Rome) on June 30, 1943 and was the first department to use hunting turned into scouts.

Technique

Fighter plane, cantilever low-wing monoplane, single-engine, single-seat all-metal structure. The metal fuselage with a half-shell structure is made up of four light alloy profiles with ovoid and corrugated bulkheads, covered in superavional, and ends with a cone inside which is housed the rear wheel, cushioned, adjustable and retractable. The wing was a cantilevered bilongherone with a biconvex profile, consisting of two dismountable semitages that were inserted into the fuselage by means of comb connections, asymmetrical semials between them to counteract the propeller torque.

The right wing had an opening of 4.32 meters and a weight of about 185 kg, while the left measured 4.52 meters of opening and weighed 168 kg.

The construction was very simple and was composed in the two semiali joined to a central trunk integral to the fuselage. The construction was made of metal truss and was composed of a bilongherone connected by 54 ribs. The coating was in duralumin with the exception of the two ailerons covered in cotton cloth. On the edge of the wingspan were installed metal flaps divided into four sections.

Special rafters for sub-aircraft loads allowed the transport of weights up to 320 kg (tanks or bombs).

The landing gear was also based on a design of the one used on the MC.202 and consisted of three main elements. The two main semicarrellis were inside the wing compartment with an inward movement, while in the aircraft of the III series on the leg of the main trolley there were some strengthening ribs. In contrast, the swiveling tail wheel was partially retractable in the fuselage terminal.

The cantilevered landing surfaces were completely metallic except for the mobile surfaces covered in canvas; variable incidence stabilizer in flight.

The pilot's cockpit was closed with a folding canopy on the right. The windbreak was equipped with a VIS 1 glass blind. The seat was armored and other armored plates protected the pilot's shoulders. Behind the pilot's seat was the support of the Saren type dipole antenna, whose other terminal was connected to the drift. The receiving-transmitting apparatus was of the Allocchio Bacchini B30 short wave non-quartz type, with an antenna first of a SAREM style and then replaced with a US-made model T.R.5043.

A RG.42 radiogoniometer model was intended as a standard installation and was identifiable by a small toroidal antenna positioned on the belly of the fuselage. The fuel was contained in four tanks all in the fuselage, one main 270 liters in the central wingpanel, two 40 liters each on the sides of the main tank and a third of 83 liters behind the shoulders of the pilot, all protected by "SEMAPE" coating (which closes the holes produced by the bullets received up to the 12.7 mm caliber).

The application of two external and detachable wing tanks of 100 or 150 liters was provided in correspondence with the attacks for the fall armament. installed the 36-liter lubricating oil tank and the water tank with a capacity of 12 liters In the ventral part of the bonnets, fixed with appropriate connections to the engine, were the two oil coolers, while the radiator the water was under the fuselage at the cockpit, the engine operated an entirely metallic propeller of Piaggio construction, Model P.20 01, tripala at constant speed, with a diameter of 3.05 meters. The engine start was electric. The injection of the petrol, before starting, was done with a pneumatic injector controlled by a deviator that was on the right of the pilot.

The air sent by the injector came from the general compressed air circuit. The compressed air was supplied by a cylinder with reducer that was filled 'air on the ground or in flight by a compressor mounted on the engine.

Two 12.7 mm Breda-SAFAT machine guns mounted above the engine cowling, synchronized and firing through the propeller blade, 400 rounds per weapon; two 20-mm winged Mauser guns with 250 rounds per weapon. The MC205V differed from the MC202, due to the different motor-propeller assembly, due to small changes in the overtake as well as the displacement of the Venturi socket, which was also connected to the pneumatic rearmament system of the on-board weapons, in some details concerning the main cart and a new series of tools and equipment introduced during production.

The Veltro had regular climb times that, despite the exuberant power, did not exceed 1,000 meters per minute except for the first km of altitude, so that between 4 and 5 km the time was 64 seconds and between 5 and 6 km was of 63 seconds. These services were not without price. Although not even comparable to the consumption of modern fighter jets, even the engines of the Second World War drank large quantities of aviation fuel.

For the Veltro, climb in seven minutes to 6 thousand meters, holding the 2,300 rpm meant a consumption variously indicated in 60-80 liters of fuel with a distance of about 30-35 km (the best speed of climb you had to 300 km/h). This means that, at this regime, the entire amount of 430 liters of fuel would have been consumed in about three quarters of an hour. Speaking of fuel, the 270-liter main tank was ahead of the pilot, and behind the engine. An ideal arrangement as it is very close to the center of gravity (even other planes, such as the Spitfire had the same solution, while it was not so for the Bf-109 or the P-51, very sensitive to changes in attitude), even with the serious potential risk that a possible fire would invest the pilotage (it seems that the thing was not in practice much feared thanks to the self-supporting tanks, while it was a serious problem with the first Spitfires).

But with the 2,300 rpm engine the plane flew for just 525 km, albeit at an excellent cruising speed of 585 km/h, consuming fuel in less than an hour. When equipped with auxiliary tanks, the data give the same values an hour and a quarter of operation and 670 km of route.

These values, however, are not congruous, because increasing the fuel by 200 liters would have meant 46% more fuel. Although the mileage autonomy could not be increased to the same extent because, with the same consumption, the aerodynamic drag slows down the aircraft, that hour depends only on the engine, which means a value of about 1 hour and a half flight. The alternative is that the plane, with only internal fuel, had only 51 minutes of autonomy.

The discrepancy, apart from the inaccuracies of detection, could be explained in various ways: the use or not of the emergency tank of 80 liters rearward to the cockpit (and two other 40 liters were on the sides), or simply the count in the calculated autonomy of the fuel needed to climb, thus deducting 60-80 liters from the total in exchange for 35 km traveled. This would leave the plane another 50-minute flight at 585 km/h, which added to the seven of the ascent actually gives the value of almost an hour of announced flight. This probably means that by increasing the fuel of 200 liters it was possible to prolong the autonomy of about 180 km (up to 670), which is directly compatible with an increase in autonomy of about 15-20 minutes, as reported by the sources: a reduction in speed with external tanks at about 550 km/h (typical of these installations, for example the Spitfire Mk V trop without and with the ventral tank has a decline of about 30 km / h), the 180 km of autonomy moreover it is about 20 minutes of flight, again in agreement with the sources.

If there was to patrol at low speeds, the Veltro could reduce the speed to 425 km/h at 1,670 rpm. This value of economic cruising speed is still high compared to many other fighters, but if it really represents the best speed in relation to consumption, the Veltro only confirms his skills as a sprinter. The autonomy in this case was 810-1.040 km for the transfer, but it is not clear whether with or without the external tanks. In hourly terms it was equivalent to 1 hour and 57 minutes/2 hours and 29 minutes.

Technical features

Dimensions and weights

- ☐ Length: 8.85 meters
- ☐ Wingspan: 10.58 meters
- ☐ Height: 3.49 meters
- ☐ Wing area: 16,80 m^2
- ☐ Wing load: 194 kg / m^2
- ☐ Empty weight: 2,524 kg
- ☐ Load weight: 3,224 kg
- ☐ Maximum takeoff weight: 3,408 kg
- ☐ Crew: 1
- ☐ Specimens: 262

Propulsion

- Motor: DB 605 A1 original twelve-cylinder inverted V; subsequently (under license) Fiat RA 1050 RC 58I "Typhoon".
- Aviation petrol: 95/100 octane
- Power:
  - ➤ 1,475 hp at 2,800 revolutions
  - ➤ 1,310 hp at 2,600 revolutions s.l.m.
  - ➤ 1,250 hp at 2,600 rpm at 5,800 meters
  - ➤ 1,355 hp at 2,800 rpm at 5,800 meters
  - ➤ 1,080 hp in maximum continuous operation (2,300 rpm) at 5,500 meters.

Performance

- Maximum speed: 642 km/h at 7,500 meters
- Cruise speed: 580 km h
- Stall speed: 158 km/h
- Take-off run: 285 meters
- Landing distance: 310 meters
- Autonomy: 950 km
- Tangency: 11,500 meters
- Ascent speed:
  - to 1,000 meters - 0.41
  - at 2,000 meters - 1.37
  - at 3,000 meters - 2.28
  - to 4,000 meters - 3.44
  - to 5,000 meters - 4.48
  - to 6,000 meters - 5.53
  - to 7,000 meters - 7.60
  - to 8,000 meters - 9.90

Armament

- Machine guns: 2 Breda-SAFAT 12.7 mm, mounted above the engine cowling, synchronized, firing through the propeller disk, 400 rounds per weapon.
- Cannons: 2 MG 151/20 caliber 20 mm, in the wings, with 250 shots per weapon
- Bombs: up to 320 kg.

Fiat 1050 RC.58

The Fiat RA.1050 RC.58 Tifone was a liquid cooled 12-cylinder V-shaped aviation engine produced by the Italian company Fiat Aviazione during the Second World War. Italian version built under license of the Daimler-Benz DB 605 was able to deliver a power equal to 1,475 HP but due to the less valuable materials available was less reliable than the German engine. In June 1939, while the prototype of the Reggiane Re.2000 fighter was carrying out the tuning cycle while waiting to be transferred to Guidonia for the official tests, it was proposed the opportunity to mount a cooled engine on the Re.2000 cell. to water of German manufacture, in place of the Piaggio P.XI radial engine.

With that engine, the Daimler-Benz DB 601, it was counted to get an increase in the performance of the aircraft thanks, in addition to the greater power available, even better aerodynamics of the engine enclosure with reduced front footprint. The idea, although not enthusiastic about the Reggiane environment, which sees the efforts to set up the series production of the Re.2000 canceled, found its concrete application in the official commission that the Ministry of Aeronautics sent on July 20th to Reggio Emilia for the construction of a prototype with a liquid-cooled engine.

The new aircraft would be called Re.2001 Falco II (but the latter name will never become official). The engine envisaged the assembly of a cooling system based on sub-radiators. When in the early months of 1940 the Re.2001 (MM409) was now ready, the construction of a second prototype with a wing with three side members and independent tanks was ordered. The development of the first model began in June, when Mario de Bernardi took to the air for the first time the aircraft equipped with the new engine (between 22 and 24 June). In July, the Re.2001 passes into the hands of Lieutenant Colonel Pietro Scapinelli who carries out the set-up before the flight to Guidonia. During the tests, some modifications are made to the engine overhaul and the cooling openings. Also the tests at Guidonia give good results, with a significant improvement in speed compared to Re.2000, 568 km/h at 5,500 meters and 540 at 4,500 meters, but these speeds will never be reached by standard aircraft because the national DB 601 are less brilliant than the original engines. The Regia Aeronautica thus confirmed the conversion of Macchi aircraft, authorizing their mass production, and almost simultaneously assigned other co-production contracts in Caproni's factories.

The Macchi MC205V began to be delivered to the operational departments at the beginning of 1943. The first department to be equipped at the end of April was the 1st Stormo CT, based in Pantelleria, which immediately began operating on the skies of the Mediterranean and in North Africa. These were stocks in naval and air convoys, either direct or coming from Tunisia. In their first outing, 22 M.C.205 faced with excellent results more numerous formations of Spitfire V and Curtiss P-40.
On 20 April 1943, about thirty Macchi M.C.205 and M.C.202 of the 1st Stormo, led by Major Di Bernardo and Captain Nioi, faced about 60 Spitfires on the Sicilian Channel. After a violent fight, the Macchi claimed the demolition of 17 Spitfire, in the face of the loss of only two fighters. According to the phonogram preserved among the operational reports of the Air Force of Sicily, "fifteen Spitfires are to be considered cut down, fourteen of which seen end up in the sea plus a crash on the ground between Capo Bon and Capo Mustafà."
Nevertheless, there has never been any evidence of allied losses during this air battle, while Italian aircraft lost three (pilots Andreoli, Fanelli and Borreo, landed in Tunisia), compared to 11 victories claimed by the allied hunters, above all from the Poles of No.145 Sqn. Other clashes occurred on April 29th and 30th, which ended with other knockdowns, and then on May 1st, again with the destruction in combat of six Spitfire and two Curtiss P-40s.
On 6 May, a formation of Macchi 205 escorted to an air convoy bound for Tunisia crashed in the Sicilian Channel with the USAAF pilots and brought down another nine P.40. The collapse of the Tunisian front and the

vulnerability of Pantelleria determined, at the beginning of May, the retreat of the 1st Wing, on the airport of Sigonella, in Sicily, with the use of the field-trampoline of Finocchiara, about 15 kilometers to south-east of Ragusa. And on the skies of Pantelleria another clash took place on 10 May with eight bombers and destroyed allied fighters. On May 19, the 1st Wing knocked down nine other Anglo-American planes. Then, in a crescendo, another five on the 22nd, four again on the 23rd and five on the 25th of the month. May 26, for the flock, is a day of great successes. In furious clashes over Sicily, 10 allied units, including fighters and bombers, are shot down.

The unit gains, for the second time in a few days, the honor of the quotation on the war bulletin.
At the beginning of July 1943, the 1st Wing was replaced by the 4th Wing, the elite unit of the Regia Aeronautica.
The 4th Stormo, which had left Africa in January 1943, had been reequipped with Macchi M.C.202 and M.C.205 on the Campoformido (10th Group) and Bresso (9th Group) airports. After a first transfer to Rome-Ciampino

airport, the flock arrived in Sicily. The Italian pilots carried out up to six missions a day. On 4 July the pilots of the 4th engaged fighting on the plain of Catania against the Allied bombers, destroying as many as 18 enemy aircrafts in repeated attacks. Particularly distinguished in the fight was the captain Franco Lucchini belonging to the 9th group who fell in combat on a Macchi 202, hit by a defensive fire attacked by a bomber, and decorated with the Gold Medal for Military Valor, and the captains Carlo Piccolomini and Luigi Caffarella together to the lieutenants Vittorio Daffara, Alvaro Querci and Mario Mecatti. On the eve of the invasion of the island, on July 9, 1943, the 4th Storm was based on the plain of Catania with a mixed endow of 10 Veltro and 38.

The flock received a complement of another 10 Veltro. But on July 14, with the first groups of Allied paratroopers operating on the Catania plain, the 4th was forced back on the airport of Crotone, in Calabria, after having fired five or six Veltro that could not be transported. On every occasion, the "Veltro" proved to be a fearsome adversary. The Macchi 205 outclassed the P-40 and was much more agile and maneuverable and equally powerful than the Spitfire V.

Up to 6,000 meters above sea level, he easily controlled the new fighter introduced by the USAAF, such as the P-47 Thunderbolt and the P- 38 Lightning. It is also known that the American pilots of the P-51 Mustang, celebrated by the Anglo-Saxon historians as "best World War II offensive fighter", feared very much the "Veltro", which revealed itself, thanks to the 20 mm Mauser cannons, a relentless destroyer of the Boeing B-17 Flying Fortresses. In June the first M.C.205V Series III were delivered, which instead of the 7.7 mm SAFAT machine guns mounted on the wings of the 20 mm Mauser cannons, proved to be very effective.

However, it is clear from documents and testimonies that some even had them earlier, even though they belonged to the Serie I (100 specimens).

In the spring of 1943 the Macchi M.C.205 were busy in the escort missions to the last Italian-German transport for Tunisia, and in the air defense of the Italian skies from an increasingly massive series of aerial bombardments. On July 9th 1943, six M.C. 205 based in Sicily intercepted a group of 20 USAAF Loockheed P-38 Lightning and P-40 Kittyhawks of the RAF.

Six Allied planes were shot down, compared to only one Italian. In mid-August the 4th Stormo fought his last great air battle, before the armistice, over the Strait of Messina and fell in collaboration with the hunters of the XXI group, 5 Spitfire and 3 Curtiss being mentioned, for the second time in a short time, from the war bulletin. Even the 3rd Wing of Lieutenant Colonel Tito Falconi, had time to bring into combat the "Veltro". While based in Cerveteri, in July 1943, the 18th Group (83rd, 85th and 95th Squadron) received some M.C.205.

The assignment of the first "Veltro" to the 3rd Stormo gave rise to a significant event because the commander Falconi wanted to honor with the "ad personam" assignment of the first 3 Macchi 205 as many pilots of his department who had distinguished themselves in combat; received the expected and desired aircraft Lieutenant Franco Bordoni Bisleri, Marshal Guido Fibbia and Sergeant Major Luigi Gorrini, all valiant hunters with assets in the abatement of various enemy aircraft.

The 3rd Stormo validly employed the "Veltro" in numerous interception missions in the sky of Lazio. On 19 July 1943, the unit attacked the formation of four USFAF troops who, at the command of General Doolittle, was destroying an entire district of Rome, knocking down two planes.

Ten days later and again on July 31st with six of the American two and four-year-olds shot down. According to Nino Arena, "On August 12, new fight with 9 enemy aircraft destroyed and then again on 13 Rome and Lazio with assets eight B-24 and P-38 shot down, other fights were lit on 19 and 21 on the border between Lazio and Campania with the demolition in competition with the XXII Autonomous hunting group, of 12 USAAF units.

On this occasion the 3rd Wing was mentioned to the honor of the war bulletin for his valiant behavior. Other fights took place on August 28th and 29th.

For the fight of August 29, the bulletin still referred to the Italians the valiant 3rd Stormo and one of its most successful pilots, the sergeant major Luigi Gorrini who had destroyed two four-engine and a twin-engine bringing to 8 the number of enemy aircraft shot down little time with the 205 and at 15 the overall victories obtained as a hunter, victories that should not be the last. After the armistice of 8 September there remained about 50 specimens in the South, including 6 Veltro arrived in flight from the Center-North, which formed the backbone of the hunting departments of the Regia Aerellica cobelligerante, mainly with 51° Stormo, operating in the Balkans up at the end of the spare parts. Some of them were even M.C.202 modified and transformed in the following model with assembly of R.A. 1050 available in the warehouses.

The transformation seems to have affected about 20 cars, but it is not clear whether the cannons were also mounted. During 1944, 18 Series III cobelligeranti were equipped with an additional fuel tank to replace the machine guns in the fuselage, taking the name of M.C.205S (Escort). In the north the Veltro constituted the first operational hunting departments of the newly formed National Aeronautic Republican (ANR), operating with the 1st "Ace of sticks" hunting group from 3 January 1944, especially against the Allied bombers.

The MCCs of the ANR, led by the German radiolocalization network that covered the entire Po valley, had to guard a vast territory, carrying out missions also in Austrian and Yugoslavian territory. The Veltro who flew to the Salò Republic destroyed a large number of Allied bombers and successfully tackled the formidable P-51D Mustang. The Italian driver with the highest number of downs, Adriano Visconti, obtained eleven of his victories in the few weeks in which he could pilot a Veltro. The first fight of the National Republican Air Force, which still operated the signs with the iron cross of the German Luftwaffe, took place on January 3, 1944 in the sky of Liguria.

The MC205, led by ace Adriano Visconti, intercepted a USAF bombing mission directed to the RIV ball bearing factories of Villar Perosa and formed by Boeing B-17 Flying Fortress bomber and the Lockheed P-38 Lightning twin-engine fighter buffer stock.

Italian fighter pilots broke down four P-38 Lightnings. Three of the US twin-engineers crashed into flames, while a quarter crashed in the Maritime Alps. The first abatement of the ANR was credited to sergeant major Francesco Cuscunà. The first fight had great prominence in the press and on the radio. Congratulations came from both Albert Kesselring and Wolfram von Richthofen. On 24 January the Macchi M.C.205 moved on two bases in Friuli. On January 28th the M.C.205 registered the first abatement of a US four-armed bomber by the ANR, for the first time with national insignia. The air victory was credited to Sergeant Marconcini. The non-commissioned officer, commander of Visconti, shot down a B-24 Liberator for training in Germany, in the southern Friuli sky. Another four-engineer was shot down, in collaboration, by three pilots, one of whom, the lieutenant Vittorio Satta, however, was in turn hit and wounded by the US bomber gunners and forced to launch himself with a parachute.

In mid-February 1944, the 1st Group was transferred to a base on the outskirts of Reggio Emilia, with the task of attacking the four-year-old allies and their escort fighters. By February 25, 1944, the 1st Group recorded 26 victories against nine losses. On 11 March there were very violent fights.

The Italian pilots claimed the demolition of 12 airplanes (the Allies registered for this mission the abatement of two B-17s and the damage of 7 others) but lost three pilots, including Lieutenant Giovanni Battista Boscutti, the remains of whose apparatus together those of the pilot were recovered sixty-three years later at Correzzola by the Romagna Air Finders group. A week later, 30 Macchi and 60 Bf 109 of JG.77, clashed with about 450 Allied bombers with their escort. The ANR pilots knocked down at least four enemy planes, but Corporal Zacharias was killed as he descended hanging from his parachute by a P-

38 pilot who deliberately took him shortly. The RAF, too, had issued provisions to machine the Axis pilots who were launched with the parachute.

On 2 May 1944, the new captain Fioroni and the "ace" captain Adriano Visconti shot down a P-51 Mustang that was attacking the "Veltro" of the second lieutenant Cucchi (intent to bring down a "Flying Fortress" B-17): first victory of our pilots at the expense of what was often called the best WWII fighter. At the end of May 1944, the number of M.C.205 available to the ANR was however already so diminished that it became necessary to gradually replace it with the Fiat G.55. Finally, due to the lack of spare parts, the few remaining Veltro specimens were relegated to training tasks. For a short time, even a German hunting group, "The ace of hearts" in the autumn of 1943, when he was in Italy found himself using C.205.

Interesting opinion of the German pilots, according to which the plane was a good fighter, although not extraordinary: had a good behavior in flight, it was fast, well armed (only in the version with the guns), but tended to tighten too much in the turns , while the supply of weapons and fuel was very long and troubled compared to their airplanes (four internal tanks instead of one only as in German Bf 109.

The radio was powerful, but unreliable due to the interferences captured. The difference in the gas controls (later adjusted to give 'throttle' pushing forward the lever and not backwards, as in normal Italian fighter) contributed to cause accidents, of which at least seven cases are known (with damages from 60% to 100%), and the loss of at least four riders. Three years after the end of the war, the Air Force Macchi obtained an order from the Royal Egyptian Air Force (REAF) for the purchase of Macchi MC205, which it used in the Arab-Israeli conflict of 1948-49, a war event that led to the birth of the state of Israel. The contract was signed on 23 June 1948.

The Varese-based company then collected all the aircraft in order to be able to return to the air and fight. The contract involved two series of 24 and 18 airplanes and between September 1948 and April 1949, Macchi delivered the first batch of 24 aircraft: 16 were former Macchi MC202 turned into "Veltro" and the others were original MC205, all equipped with sub-wing pylons for 100 kg bombs. The Egyptian "Veltro" were used in combat by the 2nd Squadron of REAF against the Israelis, but the results were controversial: according to a historian, on 7 January 1949 a Veltro destroyed a P-51D Israeli Mustang, on the other hand, three MC205 were damaged irreparably and you were seriously damaged, with the statistics that do not report if as a result of fighting or incorrect landings.

Instead, according to a more recent work, the Israelis won an overwhelming victory against the Egyptian Macchi, so much so that only between December 28, 1948 and January 5, 1949, their Spitfires and Mustangs knocked down at least five MC205Vs and destroyed two more soil without suffering any loss; probably others were lost between December 22nd and January 7th 1949, for a total of ten units. But the losses, in fact, had begun earlier: in the late forties there had been a series of attacks in Italy, which became a battleground between Arab and Israeli secret services, which also involved the aviation sector, such as when on 15 February 1947, the civil aircraft SM.95 I-ABQF exploded in flight, after taking off from Rome, carrying a princess and various Egyptian politicians.

On September 18, 1948, several bombs were placed in the aircraft hangar at Venegono, where there were also some M.C.205 ordained from Egypt.

Some did not explode, but those that succeeded destroyed a M.C.205V and three MB.308 damaging another three Veltro, with damages for 110 million lire. On 23 February 1949 the Aermacchi signed another contract with the Egyptians for 24 M.C.205 at the cost of 270,000 pounds. The 16 "Folgore" turned into M.C.205 but maintained the original armament, while the original "Veltro" were armed with the cannons MG 151/20 caliber 20 mm. The aircraft of this second batch, however, had numerous accidents, due to both the inexperience of the Egyptian pilots, and the wear and tear of the cars and especially the engines, almost always not the original Daimler Benz DB 605, but the very poor "RA- 1000 RC-58 Typhoon "built with self-sufficient materials from FIAT.

The third batch of 20 copies, despite the regular contract was refused by the Egyptians and these planes returned to Italy. The Macchi rejected by the Egyptians ended up in flight schools where they remained operational until the early fifties. The few exemplars assigned to schools, such as the Malignani Technical Institute in Udine, were saved from destruction.

At the end of the conflict, fifty or so M.C. still survived at different levels of efficiency. 205, about thirty of which, in reality, of the "Folgore" modified. A single flock, the 5th, still had the "Veltro" and some M.C. 202. In 1947, the 5th was reunited with the Spitfire IX sold by the British and passed his Macchi to the Hunting School of Galatina / Lecce.

The last "Veltro" will fly again until 1951, in the flight school of Brindisi. Now worn out by innumerable war and school-hunting flights, the last Macchi 205 will still serve for years as target-shapes for the training of the armourers, until their complete destruction and scrapping. Three "Veltro" still exist, to date, one of which was restored by the then Aeronautica Macchi and put in conditions to fly. This example participated in numerous air shows until the end of 1986. Today it is preserved by today's Alenia Aermacchi at the entrance of the building of the general management in the Venegono plant.

Commander Adriano Visconti

Adriano Visconti di Lampugnano was an ace of Italian aviation during the Second World War and commander of the 1st hunting group "Ace of sticks". He enrolled in the Regia Aeronautica as a student of the REX Course of the Air Force Academy on October 21st 1936 and obtained the military pilot's license at the aviation school of Caserta.

He continued his training on the Breda Ba.25 and on the IMAM Ro.41 and, in 1939, he was assigned to the 159th Squadron of the 50th Stormo d'Assalto (department specialized in ground attack). In June 1940, at the outbreak of the war, Visconti was transferred with his department in North Africa, at the airport of Tobruk, where he fought flying over the Breda Ba.65 and the Caproni Ca.310. Between June and December 1940, he was decorated with two Silver Medals for Military Valor and a Bronze Medal. In January 1941 Visconti was transferred to the 76th Squadron of the 54th Earthly Hunting Storm where he was trained on the flight on the Macchi M.C.200 fighter, then operating on the island of Malta and in the African skies with the Macchi M.C.202.

On April 29, 1943, during the last major air crash before the fall of Tunisia, the then Lieutenant Visconti led twelve Macchi M.C.202 of the 7th Group to the sixty attack between Supermarine Spitfire and Curtiss P-40. Visconti brought down a P-40, while four others were credited to other pilots of the 54th Wing. Visconti was proposed for the granting of a Silver Medal for military valor that was granted on June 10, 1948, three years after the death of the Italian ace.

Later, promoted to the rank of captain, he became commander of the 310th Squadron Hunting

Aerofotografica, specialized in air-reconnaissance and equipped with Macchi M.C.205 in a special version modified to Guidonia. After the armistice of September 8, 1943, Visconti joined the Italian Social Republic and actively participated in the establishment of the National Republican Air Force commanding the 1st Squadron and, after being promoted to the rank of major in May 1944, the 1st Hunting Group "Ace of sticks".

Until the end of the war, Visconti fought defending northern Italy from the attacks of the Anglo-American bombers using different types of aircraft: Macchi M.C.202, M.C.205 and Messerschmitt Bf 109G-10.

The first fight on this last type of aircraft took place on March 14th. Visconti, commander of the 1st Group, with another 16 Messerschmitt, intercepted, on Lake Garda, a formation of B-25 Mitchell of the 321th Bomber Group, which came after the bombing of the railway bridge of Vipiteno. The P-47 Thunderbolt escorts also attacked the Italian Messerschmitt. During the fight, Visconti attacked the 1/Lt Thunderbolt frontally.

Charles C. Eddy, claiming the slaughter, but the commander of the 1st group was hit and wounded in the face by the splinters of his windshield and forced to launch. On March 15, the ANR attributed the victory to Visconti and the secretariat forwarded the practice to request the "Premio del Duce", the 5,000 lire that belonged to the abattoir of a single engine. In fact, the P-47 of the American Eddy returned to the base of Pisa with the damaged aircraft and was again operational on 2 April following another mission. On April 29, 1945, in Gallarate, Adriano Visconti signed the surrender of his department, the 1st Hunting Club "Asso di sticks" countersigned by representatives of the Regia Aeronautica, the National High Liberation Committee (CLNAI), the National Liberation Committee (CNL) and 4 partisan leaders (including Aldo Aniasi "Iso", then mayor of Milan and then deputy and minister).

The agreement (later betrayed) guaranteed the freedom for the officers and officers of the Group, the personal safety of all the officers, as well as the commitment to surrender to the Italian or Allied military authorities, as prisoners of war.

The 60 officers and 2 auxiliaries were taken to the barracks of the "Savoia Cavalleria", formerly the headquarters of the Republican National Guard, then occupied by the "Redi" and "Rocco" garbaldine brigades. The prisoners had been placed in a first room when a partisan ordered Visconti to follow him. Sub-lieutenant Valerio Stefanini, aide of Visconti followed him. Around 2:00 pm, while the officers were taken to another room where brande had been prepared, two sudden gusts were heard. According to Luftwaffe's attaché to the Republican Air Force, Colonel von Ysemburg, who was then present, the two, Visconti and Stefanini, were hit behind by machine guns.

Visconti was finished with two pistol shots on the back of the head. The news of the execution was subsequently communicated to the remaining prisoners. Shooting was a partisan of Russian nationality, bodyguard of the partisan Aldo Aniasi "Iso", commander of the "Redi" garibaldine brigade. The partisan was then indicted and immediately acquitted as a legitimate act of war, having occurred before May 8, 1945, the date of the official end of hostilities in Europe. Visconti was buried in the Musocco cemetery in Milan in Camp 10, called Campo dell'Onore, along with hundreds of members of the Italian Social Republic who fell for those tragic days, many of whom remained anonymous. 10 airline victories in the Royal Air Force (1940-1943) have been officially accredited, number reported by Visconti himself in his flight booklet. The 1st hunting group recognizes him instead 14. According to some, there are 26 aerial victories: 19 obtained by fighting in the Regia Aeronautica and 7 in the National Republican Air Force of the Italian Social Republic.

125

Sergeant Luigi Gorrini

Luigi Gorrini was one of the last great aviation boards of the Regia Aeronautica, Gold Medal for Military Valor.
During the Second World War he was credited with 19 shot down planes, 15 with the Regia Aeronautica and 4 with the Republican National Air Force, but some authors awarded him 24, and 9 damaged, between Curtiss P-40, Spitfire, P-38 Lightning , P-47 Thunderbolt and B-17 "Flying Fortresses". His victories were achieved at the controls of the Fiat C.R.42 biplane and the Macchi M.C.202 Folgore and M.C.205 Veltro monoplane. Gorrini was the main ace on the Veltro, with which he knocked down 14 enemy planes and damaged six of them. After his childhood he enrolled in the Regia Aeronautica at 20 years, in 1937. After completing the pilotage course at the School of Specialization of Castiglione del Lago, Gorrini applied to be assigned to the 3rd Wing, framed in the 2nd Air Division Borea based at the Turin-Mirafiori airport.
On 17 June 1939 he was transferred to the ward and integrated into the 85th Squadron of the 18th Group with the rank of pilot sergeant. Served with this unit until the armistice of Cassibile, September 8, 1943. Then entered the ranks of the National Republican Air Force (ANR) almost to the end of the conflict. Gorrini arrives in North Africa in January 1941 at the controls of a Fiat C.R.42.
"The CR 42 - recalls the pilot - was a car already outdated - a canvas biplane, without armor, with radio equipment and malfunctioning oxygen systems - it was a very nice device as far as handling, armed with 2 machine guns of 12 , 7, effective machine guns, but the British had 8, although the size 0.30 ".

Despite the limitations of the CR42, it is with this biplane that Gorrini, in Libya, gets his first air victory on April 16, 1941. While in flight of protection in the sky of Derna, in Cyrenaica, he intercepts two of the first Bristol Beaufighter as soon as they arrive in the Mediterranean theater, heading towards Ftheja Camp No. 1, the base of its 85th Squadron.

The English patrol is almost out of range, but Gorrini opens fire from 7-800 meters. It hits the tip of the right wing of the head Beaufighter, while quickly closing the distance, thanks to the speed accumulated with the dive. The other aircraft goes off with a sharp turn while the first Bristol is now on the field of Ftheja. From 250 meters Gorrini centers it with two successive gusts and the British plane immediately crashes south of the field. He is then attributed an individual killing and a « damaged ». 1,100 shots are fired.

On 29 May Gorrini, again in flight of protection, sighted two Bristol Blenheim on the port of Benghazi. After a beat of three thousand meters he attacked the head plane. He fired a 500-meter burst and hit the patrol leader, despite the defensive fire of the two enemy twin-engines. The head of the Bristol, repeatedly hit, fell into the waters of the port. He then went in pursuit of the other Blenheim, unloading all the blows that remained, but the British twin-engine could get away unscathed. Repatriated with his department, August 29 is in Caselle Torinese to begin training on new monoplane fighters, the Fiat G.50 and the Macchi M.C.200.

To continue the training, Gorrini and his 18th group moved first to Mirafiori and then to Ciampino Sud, where training on the new fighters ended on December 10, when his unit, equipped with the Macchi M.C. 200, flew first to Lecce and then to the new base of Araxos, in Greece. During the winter of 1941-42, Gorrini carried out escort flights in convoys between Italy and Greece. On December 17, in the aerial area around the port of Argostoli, in Kefalonia, intercepts two Bristol Blenheim completely painted black. Attack the head one by hitting it repeatedly and then machine the other.

The two Blenheim, they separate disappearing in the clouds and Gorrini is credited with a plane shot down and the damage of the second. Gorrini has no other opportunities for confrontation with allied aircraft and repatriation with the 18th, April 25, 1942.

Back in Italy, Gorrini and the other pilots of the 18th were trained to pilot the M.C.200 in the configuration of the fighter-bomber. The training lasted until mid-July, when his unit flew to North Africa to reach the other 3rd Wing Group, on the 23rd, at Abu Haggag's advanced airport. From that advanced base, Gorrini carries out escort missions for Axis ships and attacks on the ground, with the new "Manzolino" bombs. When, in October, the 4th Stormo, now worn out, was withdrawn, he handed over his Macchi M.C. 202 at the 3rd Wing. Thus, from the 20th of that month, the 18th Group could resume its hunting department duties.

"Finally, with the Macchi 202 we had a competitive airplane, of course when they threw us swarms of P-40 and Spitfire on the offensive, this car could not do too much." The Spitfire was a very hard bone. He had a bunch of machine guns, plus two 20 mm guns and he was also faster, the 202 was much lower in speed and armament ".

On January 2, 1943, the entire 3rd Wing, equipped with Macchi M.C.202 transferred from the 4th Stormo, took off to face two formations of Douglas DB.7 Boston and B-25 Mitchell, escorted by Spitfire and P-40. In the air battle that ensued, Gorrini knocked down a Curtiss P-40E Kittyhawk of R.A.F., which crashed west of Sirte. Soon after, he attacked and damaged a Spitfire that was chasing another Macchi. Gorrini had fired a total of 880 shots but also his plane had been hit: there were 12 holes on his fuselage. Nine days later, while he is escorting, with other pilots of the 3rd Stormo, to MC200 fighter-bomber in action on British airports in the area of the Uadi Tamet, he breaks down one of the Spitfires of the British ace Flying Officer Neville Duke of the 92nd Squadron and damage another. On the morning of February 26, Gorrini took off to escort a formation of Junkers Ju 87 Stuka to attack allied armed forces in the area of Ksar-Ghilane and, subsequently, to machine enemy troops on the ground. In the afternoon, with Lieutenant Melis and two other pilots of his squadron, he intercepts four Allied planes on Kebili, Tunisia. In the fight that followed, Gorrini claimed the downing of a Hawker Hurricane IID, armed with 40mm Vickers. At the beginning of 1943, Gorrini is one of the pilots charged with transferring the French Dewoitine D.520 war fighters to Italy, to defend the mother country.

"I transferred several dozen Dewoitine D. 520 from various French airports and from the Toulouse factory," recalled Gorrini. "At that time, when we were still flying with the Macchi MC.200, it was a good car, even if not exceptional, compared to the" Saetta "was superior only in one point: its armament with the 20 mm Hispano-Suiza HS cannon 404. "

Gorrini, who had obtained four confirmed victories since February 1943 and an unconfirmed one, obtains, at the beginning of the summer, one of the three Macchi "Veltro" Macchi, assigned to the 3rd Stormo (the other two are entrusted to ace Franco Bordoni Bisleri and to Marshal Guido Fibbia), revealing his unusual skills as a fighter pilot during the defense of Rome. His series of aerial victories began on 19 July 1943, the day of the first bombing in the history of Rome. That day, Gorrini comes into action with another 37 pilots of the 3rd Wing against the 930 bombers and US Air Force escort fighters involved in the Crosspoint Operation. It takes off from Cerveteri with its 85th squadron, on a Macchi M.C. 202. Off the coast of Ostia, attack the first formation of B-17 Flying Fortress.

"I saw him fall, I would not know the exact time because the fight was a matter of minutes, I made three or four attacks against this four-engine, I tried to shoot him in front, three-quarters, and I saw a nice moment go down ... He fell in the area between Sezze and Littoria ".

According to other sources, on July 19, he broke down, in the course of a single mission, a quadratotor Consolidated B-24 Liberator bomber and a twin-engine fighter Lockheed P-38 Lightning (another damaged P-38). The following day repeats:

"In another fight, the next day, Tuesday 20, another fell on Neptune's airport ... It was a B-17, it still had bombs, I cut a wing after two passes, but this time I had the MC 205, and I saw a good moment his right wing detach from the fuselage and the revolving engines and the wing that went away and so went into the screw. "

Immediately afterwards he was attacked by a P-38 escort:

"I discarded, he passed me in front of his face ... and with all his weapons, machine guns and cannons of 20, I planted him a gun. The fall of the fascist government has no decisive effect on the morale of the Regia Aeronautica.

"After July 25, despite the arrest of Benito Mussolini, the morale of my unit remained high and my personal willingness to take action was total Despite the reverses suffered at that time, our Flock was the only one still fully Operation for Combat My section had been set aside for the defense of Rome Most of the men of the Royal Air Force were not interested in politics or parties They were in love with the flight and determined to defend their homeland and give their lives , if necessary, in an attempt to stop the bombing of Italian cities".

On August 13, Rome suffers the second of the two heaviest bombings in its history. Gorrini and the few other pilots of the 83rd and 85th squadrons in defense of the holy city rise in flight from the "strips" of Palidoro, to intercept the 409 - between bombers and escort fighters - aircraft of the Twelfth Air Force. At 20 kilometers across the Anzio, at 7,000 meters, intercepts the first formation of B-17 with the P-38 escort. Gorrini, on a Macchi M.C. 205, attacks one of the four engines left behind with respect to the others. After several attacks, the B-17 crashes: "He went to fall into the sea between Neptune and Littoria, but I could not follow his fall because the Lightning attacked me from above."

Gorrini manages to disengage, but during his second sortie against the third wave of bombers, is attacked by escort fighters and is forced to launch from 2,000 meters on the area Littoria-Sezze, where it lands unharmed. According to other sources, still on August 13, off Ostia, plunges another B-24, but is hit by the bomber's gunner and must launch with the parachute on Sezze. On August 26 throws down a Supermarine Spitfire and, the next day, under the blows of the 20mm guns of his Macchi M.C.205, fall two B-24 attacking Cerveteri.

One of the Mauser cannons, overheated, explodes damaging a wing but, despite running out of fuel, on the river Volturno, manages to fly his hunt as a glider, to the German base of Pratica di Mare. Three days later, on 29 August, he breaks down two P-38s and damages two more. The next day he destroys another four-engine B-17 and is mentioned in the war bulletin. On August 31st, his last fight took place under the banner of the Regia Aeronautica.

Taking off from the airport of Palidoro with its 85th squadron, it crashes at 8,500 meters, in the sky of Naples, with the Supermarine Spitfire escorted by a flock of U.S.A bombers. Knock down a Supermarine Spitfire (three other British fighters are declared shot down by his squadron) and damage another P-38 but his plane is hit and must make a crash landing. Seriously wounded, he is hospitalized, where he surprises him on September 8th. At the date of the armistice of Cassibile, Gorrini had supported 132 fights, achieved 15 knockdowns and 9 probable, had been wounded twice, had been mentioned several times on the war bulletin and had been proposed 6 times for decorations, obtaining 2.

Gorrini , like other 6,996 other volunteers, responds to the call of Lt. Col. Ernesto Botto and reaches Northern Italy to continue fighting against the Allies.

"After having flown for three years side by side with the German pilots, on the English Channel, in North Africa, Greece, Egypt, Tunisia and - finally - on my homeland, I had made friends with some of them, in particular JG 27 .. I did not want to do the weather vane, to say that, and maybe shoot on my German friends. Furthermore, I wanted to protect the cities of Northern Italy from indiscriminate bombings as far as possible ".

On 23 December 1943 he enlisted in the National Republican Air Force, in the 1st hunting group "Ace of sticks". On January 30th of that month, in the sky of Grado, at the controls of a Macchi M.C.205 he felled a P-47 "Thunderbolt" of the 325th Fighter Group escorted by American bombers of the 15th Air Force. The next morning he intercepts and plunges a reconnaissance P-38 based in Bari Palese into the Comacchio lagoon. March 11 throws down a four-engine B-17 again. On 6 April, north of Zadar, Gorrini plunges his second P-47, but is in turn knocked down by a Thunderbolt, managing to save himself with a parachute. Gorrini gets his last victory two months later, May 24, 1944.

That day takes off with Lieutenant Vittorio Satta, again on M.C.205, to intercept, on the dial of Parma-Fidenza, a formation of B-24 directed to the south. In the sky of Colorno, the two pilots of the A.N.R. attack the two American tail bombers. Gorrini hits in full, the first pass, the Liberator, whose engines ignite and whose cart is lowered for damage suffered, but Satta is attacked by two P-47 that knocked him down before Gorrini can intervene. And it is always one of these heavy fighter to hit and hurt him severely, on June 15, 1944.

"My last fight was when I was knocked down, it was the fifth time, in Reggio Emilia, with the 205. I have always had in the RSI available the 205, sometimes the Fiat G.55.They gave us the very late alarm and we left, but we could not get enough quota and fell on us: they brought me down to Fogliano. I opened the parachute, but in the fall on the ground I violently beat my back and lost consciousness: around there were the peasants with the pitchfork that maybe they believed me to be an Englishman or an American.The Major Visconti came to pick me up and with his car took me to our doctor, who visited me and sent me to the hospital in Reggio .. The doctor in Reggio gave me a license: I was badly reduced, near a nervous breakdown, and I went home. "When I returned, it was all over."

Gorrini will not fly again during the war. His career as a fighter pilot ends here. He himself synthesized his career as follows: "212 fights, 24 individual air victories, 5 parachutes." During the war he was awarded two Bronze medals for Military Valor and the first and second class German Iron Cross. In 1958 he was awarded the Gold Medal for Military Valor, the only ANR driver to have

received the highest honor of the Italian armed forces. Despite the initial opposition of the Allied Command, he managed to enter the ranks of the newly formed Air Force. His last unit was the 50th Stormo, but for the appointment as an officer he had to wait for retirement, in 1979. As for every pilot, some of Gorrini's downsides, albeit supported by testimonies, are not confirmed by the registers of the air forces involved . Furthermore, all the abatements are known
Italian pilots are unofficial, as the Regia Aeronautica - unlike the Allied and German air forces - did not keep official records of the victories of its pilots, preferring to attribute the slaughter to the entire group. He lived in his native country until his death in 2014 at the age of 97.